YOUTH CULTURE
AND THE GOSPEL

Church work with
Youth

I. Title

YOUTH CULTURE AND THE GOSPEL

——— ✳ ———

Pete Ward

Marshall Pickering
An Imprint of HarperCollinsPublishers

First published in Great Britain in 1992 by Marshall Pickering

Marshall Pickering is an imprint of
HarperCollins*Religious*,
Part of HarperCollins*Publishers*,
77–85 Fulham Palace Road,
Hammersmith, London W6 8JB

Printed and bound in Great Britain by
HarperCollins Manufacturing, Glasgow

A catalogue record for this book
is available from the British Library

To Arnie and Mary Lou Jacobs
thank you

CONTENTS

Acknowledgements   9

Part I   Getting the Background in Focus   11

1 Forever Young   13
2 Meanwhile in Church   22
3 Picturing Jesus   34

Part II   Altered Images   45

4 Getting to Know Young People   47
5 Building Up an Understanding   57
6 Friendship   74
7 Music   82
8 Magazines   92
9 Sex   102

Part III   The Big Picture   113

10 Why Doesn't Jesus Preach the Gospel?   115
11 When Jesus Becomes Real (i) Starting from the Positive 124
12 When Jesus Becomes Real (ii) Starting with Problems   135

Part IV   So What?   151

13 True Disciples   153
14 Reading the Bible   163
15 Relating to the Church   173

Outroduction   183
Bibliography   185
Index   191

ACKNOWLEDGEMENTS

Writing this book has only served to show me, even more clearly, that I have learned so much from the young people who have accepted me as their friend over the last few years. My debt to these young people is very great indeed. I can't thank them all by name individually but it has to be said that this book owes its life to them.

My colleagues in Oxford Youth Works – Kenny Wilson, Bob and Sherry Dupee, Judith Levermore and Tina Freimuth – have been over the years not only an inspiration, but also a joy to be associated with. The ideas in this book belong to a large extent to them. I hope I have been a good spokesperson for them, and if I have not, then they are not really to blame. I would also like to thank the Trainees who have been through our Nine Month Course whilst I was working on this material. Their questions and insights have helped me to sort out my muddled ideas on more than one occasion.

I would also like to acknowledge the great debt I owe to the late Ann Ind. She encouraged me to continue with this book when I was on the point of giving up. Her remarkable insight and encouragement will be a loss I will continue to feel.

Along the way a number of people have read this book and helped me to knock it into shape; they include: Sam Adams, Christine Whitell, Kaz Mayes, Tim Dakin, Kes Summersgill, Simon Law, Tess Ward, Bob, Judith and Sherry. Their advice has been invaluable.

Finally I would like to thank Arnie and Mary Lou Jacobs for their amazing generosity and faithfulness. It was Arnie and Mary Lou who got me started on this journey, and for that I will never be able to thank them enough.

Oxford 1991   PETE WARD

PART I

*

*Getting
the Background in Focus*

1

Forever Young

As a Christian Youthworker I live in two worlds. The first world is created by young people themselves. This is the continually changing bright and alive world of youth culture. When I'm in this world young people regularly astound me with their creativity, their anger, their sensitivity, their hope and their hopelessness. The other world that I live in is similar; it's the world of the Gospel. In this world Jesus makes people new, vibrant and alive. He meets them as Good News and they "kick start" into action, transformed to live new lives. The one world I see on the streets, in the schools and at rock concerts. The other world I read about in the Bible. From where I'm standing these two worlds look remarkably alike. They have so much in common and so much to give each other, yet they seldom seem to meet in any significant way. This book is an attempt to show how these two worlds can come together.

What follows is a reflection on my own work amongst young people in Oxford in the light of the Good News of Jesus. I've tried as much as possible to talk about real young people in real situations; theories are only much use when you can say that you've tried them out. But this book is also meant to help anyone who wants to try to reach out to young people in the name of Christ.

I don't make any apology for starting with a look at youth culture. Experience tells me this is the place to start because this is where young people are at. But experience has also shown me that exciting things start to happen when young people meet Jesus within their own culture. So this book is also written out of the strong belief that this is precisely where Jesus wants to meet young people. In fact, this is an essential part of the Good News; Jesus meets people where they are, in ways they can understand.

Youth Culture

Britain is a world leader in youth culture. You don't have to think very long to come up with a list of amazing young home-grown "creations". Imagine for a minute the threatening chic of the Teddy Boy, or the gravity-defying spikes of a Punk Rocker, or maybe you prefer the shaven head of the Skinhead, or the black make-up of a Goth. The originality and creativity of these groups is very striking. How many of us would ever dream up the idea of wearing plastic bin liners and sticking safety pins through our nose? How many of us would think of taking a brand new pair of Levi 501's and ripping holes in the knees? If we can just stop ourselves saying, "Well, who would want to?", and start to admire the fact that somewhere a group of young people did these things for the first time, we might be on the edge of discovering something of the marvel of these kind of groups.

But they're not all like that

Whenever I go and talk about youth culture to groups around the country, somewhere along the line someone stands up and says, "Young people in our area aren't like that". I admit I've started by mentioning the more spectacular, and therefore more noticeable youth cultures, but it doesn't stop with them. The majority of young people don't dress in ways that are too outrageous, but this does not mean that they are not part of a group. Indeed, if you ask young people about their local school they will tell you all of the various groups that exist there. Allegiances are announced by wearing the "right" pair of trainers, or that particular badge advertising that particular rock band, and then there is that one way of having your hair cut so it looks like it "should". Even those who claim not to be part of one of the groups in the school, hang around with friends who think the same, and dress roughly the same, as they do.

Of course these groups of young people are usually not the first to dress that way. Most copy what they see on the telly, or in magazines, or what they see others doing. But does this make it any less important? After all the main point, surely, is that they choose to adopt something which they can make their own. Choosing one pair of trainers rather than another is not simply a matter of artistic judgement, nor is it solely a question of value for money. Nine times out of ten the choice of such an item identifies the wearer with the group that wears that type of trainer. It is a way of placing yourself relative to the rest of your friends at school: "Look, I'm in this group 'cos I'm wearing these trainers."

Get my meaning

Youth cultures have always been about certain consumer items being used to convey new meanings. One example of this is the Mods who in the 60s started to ride Italian scooters. Now my Granddad used to have a Lambretta scooter and it was a slow, safe, and sensible machine. But in the hands of the Mods it was transformed into a glorious symbol of the freedom of youth. Mirrors would spring out at all angles, chrome racks and accessories would be added, and to top it all a long aerial with a small leopardskin pendant would hang from the back. These young people had taken my Granddad's scooter and transformed it into something full of new meaning.

From the outside it's hard for us to understand how a simple everyday item like a scooter or a pair of trainers could have such significance. To us the meaning stays hidden, but to young people the messages are obvious. The other day a boy I know came round to my place wearing a long-cut tee-shirt with a mystical "New-Age"-type symbol on the front. His mates started to pull his leg. "You Casual," they said. That particular kind of tee-shirt carried an identifiable meaning for the group. He knew it when he bought it and the group picked it up as soon as they saw him wearing it.

When we talk about "youth culture" these commonly understood meanings are an essential part of the scene. Young people live in a sharply divided world which has its own recognized language based upon consumer items like trainers or scooters. Put like this, it sounds fairly simple to grasp; if young people can learn this language then youthworkers should be able to as well. This is in a sense true, but several factors complicate the picture somewhat. The first of these is the sheer number of groups in Britain at the moment. No longer do things so neatly divide into two main groups like "Mods and Rockers" or "Skinheads and Hippies"; today there are all sorts of different groups.

So many groups

The variety of youth cultures to be found in our cities and towns at the moment is bewildering. The other day I walked into the centre of Oxford, and on the way I made a note of all the different types of young people I met.

The first thing to catch my eye was the haircut of a young man sitting on a bench. He had the tallest Mohican I had ever seen! I'm colour-blind, but this bright blue pile of hair registered with even my dulled senses. As if to counteract the colour of the hair, this present-day "punk" was dressed in a uniform black. His appearance was a bit worn and dirty as if he had spent the last few months sleeping rough. Just a few yards up the road I noticed, coming towards me, a group of three young lads. They were walking fast with their arms swinging in a confident – almost challenging – way. On their feet they all had "Timberland"-style walking boots. These are tan coloured, brushed leather boots with yellow laces; every shop in town currently has them prominently displayed in their windows. All wore the latest kind of jeans. These are very baggy in the leg; in fact they are so baggy that you could probably make two pairs of normal jeans out of them! To complement the uniformity of the boots and jeans the three young lads sported the brightest, most psychedelic hooded tops I have seen.

A bit further on I came across a small group of young people standing outside a newsagent's. One of the young men in the group had the sides of his head shaved and the rest of his hair was left unwashed for months, so that the hair had matted and formed dreadlocks. He was wearing on his feet what looked like a pair of old gardening boots. They were not laced up at all, and the toe on his right boot had started to come away from the sole. With an old pair of torn jeans, a patched, ripped and filthy old greatcoat, and a small white dog balancing precariously on his shoulders, the whole impression was of someone who had stepped out of London's Victorian underworld. Next to him was a young girl who matched him for Dickensian charm, although round her waist, over the top of a pair of baggy Indian leggings, she wore a flowery summer skirt. Jogging past this group came a clean-cut-looking girl. Her hair was in a ponytail tied high up on her head so that it tick-tocked merrily from side to side as she ran along. She was dressed in a matching blue cotton tracksuit, and as she swept past I could see that on the back of the tracksuit top, in bold white letters, were the initials O.U.W.B.C.

Coming out of a record shop in the centre of town I noticed two different groups of young people. First out were two young-looking lads. They each wore tee-shirts which advertised in graphic detail the name of their favorite bands: Iron Maiden and Anthrax. They, too, wore jeans, but these were very tight and looked as if they were clean on that morning. On their feet they each wore leather baseball boots. Not far behind them came two other lads. These were the first black teenagers that I had seen that day, and I was interested to note that they too were wearing baseball boots. But these boots were of the more flashy kind, and each boot had been laced so that the large padded inner tongue was pointing up proudly displaying the name of its expensive make to the watching world. The lads wore track suits of the slinky silk variety with fluorescent yellow stripes down the arms and the legs. Down one side of the tracksuit bottoms the word "Puma" was written in the same bright yellow material.

Always changing

The fact that in a small city like Oxford there could be so many different groups of young people is extraordinary, but this is not the end of it all. By the time that you read this most of these styles of dress will almost definitely have died out in Oxford. Young people do not stay young, they grow up. Youth culture is a living phenomenon that is always changing. In most schools there is a new generation every four years, so styles of dress will always be on the move. As a youthworker this can be a bit disconcerting. You're just getting in tune with a particular "culture" and suddenly it's all out of date. The new project that you have taken two years to get funded and set up is ignored, simply because it's old hat!

The reverse of this, of course, is that young people are always being creative. Every new generation is making its own particular kind of expression. Youth culture is "for ever young" (to use the words of a famous old hippy). This means there is always a certain amount of energy coming from young people which makes youthwork such an exciting proposition. But the complexity does not stop here, because there are considerable variations between different parts of the country.

Mods might have died out years ago in North London, but in North Wales they may still be a regular part of the scene. Skinhead gangs might be busy beating people up in Durham, but are nowhere to be seen in Manchester. Regional variations such as these are all part of the rich pattern of life we see amongst young people. A while ago a young curate told me about a group of young people who hang out in his churchyard in Swindon. They wear black balaclava hoods and military-style combat jackets. Imagine the shock regular churchgoers get on a dark evening when they run into people looking like they are part of an IRA hit squad! This group was a new one on me, but regional variations in youth cultures are not the end of the complexities that make up the world of young people.

The world in our cities

Britain is a multi-cultural country. All of the shops in my local area are owned by Asian businessmen and women, and the restaurants are run by Chinese, West Indian, Italian, Greek and Asian people. Within two minutes' walk of where I work there is a Mosque, a Jewish Synagogue, an Asian-led Christian church and a black-led church. Of course this is not a unique situation in this respect; the same could be said of many of our towns and cities.

When we come to talk about youth culture it's clear that the children of these people are all struggling to establish their identity. On the one hand they have the culture of their school friends and adopted country, and on the other they have the rich heritage of their community and home. It is not easy to grow up being Asian and British. Asian boys I talk to, given their admiration for the likes of Imran Khan and Sunil Gavaskar, would fail Norman Tebbitt's famous "cricket" test. But, at the same time, many of them are proud to be British. What we shouldn't miss is the fact that amongst these groups exciting new youth cultures can arise.

Black music both from America and Britain has always been a part of youth culture. When Elvis Presley hit the scene with a fusion of white country and black music much of what we recognize as youth culture was born. We're all fairly familiar with rock and roll's roots in black gospel and blues music but Asian young people in Britain are doing a similar thing. Bhungra Beat mixes Western dance music with Indian music, synthesizers and electric guitars played alongside traditional Asian instruments. On top is a vocal line, sometimes in English, but more often in Punjabi or Bengali, sung in the wonderful style of Indian song.

An exciting world

It's a crime that Christians are so often quick to condemn young people. If we could just stop being threatened by the way they choose to dress, or act, or by the music they listen to, maybe we could see in youth culture much that mirrors the desires and concerns of the Christian Gospel.

The world of young people is so exciting. There is so much to admire and marvel at as generation after generation find new ways to express their particular viewpoint on life. The immense variety I have so far described is in itself a testimony to the creativity of young people. Of course some of this is misdirected, but on the other hand there is so much that is good. Young people have been in the forefront in opening our eyes to the importance of the environment, the threat of nuclear war, the need for a spiritual life, the value of relationships and friendship, the problems of famine and injustice throughout the world, and, not least, the plight of many who are finding life tough in Britain today whether through unemployment, homelessness or the threat of AIDS.

When I turn to the Bible I see similar concerns being expressed. There doesn't seem to be much conflict between the kinds of things God would like to see happening in our world and the hopes and aspirations of many young people I know. Jesus isn't a strange alien character when seen through the eyes of youth culture; in fact in many ways he seems to be very much at home. These young people live in the kind of exciting world that Jesus likes to be part of.

So what's the problem?

The tragedy is that Jesus never seems to get the opportunity to take his rightful place in this exciting world. Of course Jesus is very much involved in young people's lives; it's just they do not recognize him. His presence remains hidden, because young people rarely get the chance to hear about Jesus in ways they can relate to. The problem here is that there is a communication gap.

As Christians we are charged with sharing the Good News of Jesus in the world. This, of course, brings us to the Church. The contrast between the world of youth culture and the world of the Church could not be greater, and we'll look at this contrast in the next chapter. But at this point it is best simply to say that there is great suspicion on both sides. Young people have rejected the Church with a resounding "no". The Church for its part has at best struggled to keep pace and understand, and at worst has shouted loudly about the evils of the present generation.

This is a situation which must not continue. There is a deep need for this failure in communication and breakdown in relationships to be overcome and the change needs to start with those of us in the Church. The responsibility lies firstly with those of us who are Christian. We should try to demonstrate how the world of youth culture can be enriched and transformed by the Gospel. This can only be done if we are willing first to meet, then to understand and finally to value not simply young people themselves, but also the cultures they have chosen to adopt. In taking this path we will only be following a way Jesus has already trod, when he became a human being and lived amongst us. We need to learn again to place our feet in his footmarks. Isn't this exactly what he would want?

2

Meanwhile in Church

The other week I took some young people along to our local church. I probably need to explain: my local church would normally be considered a fairly lively go-ahead place; we sing modern choruses and all that kind of thing. I was really interested to see how these young people, most of whom had never been to church before, reacted to the service. The first thing that was immediately obvious was that they felt uncomfortable. The people in church were different from them. They looked around the building and nobody else had a Mohican haircut or were wearing dirty old ripped jeans, or even dreadlocks and dyed hair (except for the odd blue rinse that was). Nobody likes to stand out in the crowd and these young people simply by their appearance looked as if they didn't belong.

But it wasn't only how they were dressed that made them feel awkward. The way our church is arranged means that everyone sits in rows facing the front. This was not only formal, and therefore uncomfortable, it was also quite strange. The young people normally sit in a circle round a table when they get together at the local pub or when they are hanging around in each other's homes. They would usually sit so that they could at least see each other's faces; they're into being together with each other. Of course so are the people at my local church, but it just comes out a different way.

When the service got underway, uncomfortable first impressions were just reinforced. In the first place, from start to finish we were listening to one person talking from the front. There didn't seem to be any room in the service for people to ask questions or to disagree. This also seemed strange to the young people. They like to talk about things and argue it out, they feel that they should respect each other's views and are interested to find out what each of them thinks on any topic. Then we came to music. Interestingly enough music is crucially important to both the church people and to this group of young people. My local church is quite trendy in many ways; we sing all the new songs with a "music group" leading us on guitars, but to the young people this music was a bit "comic". It wasn't that the music was out of date or unfamiliar to them, it was just very difficult for them to take it seriously. Somehow all the rhythms and tunes came over as the kind of music that you want to do funny dances and actions to. But this was not the only thing about the music they felt to be somehow strange. Many songs split the congregation up into men and women, you know the sort of thing, the men sing one part and the women sing another. Commenting afterwards the young people said they found the way that women simply echoed what the men sang was very "sexist". In fact during the service the group staged their own protest by the girls singing the first part and the guys following their lead!

Young people and the Church

Taking this group along to church "cold" was probably always going to produce some problems, but it did serve to highlight some points of tension that we should look at.

The first point is that the church service was so passive. There we all were sitting in rows listening to someone talking from the front for the best part of an hour. It's no wonder the young people found the experience dull, so little was expected of them. There was no real challenge to think or discuss anything – all we had to do was sit still and keep quiet. The service leaders and preacher had already done all the work and all we had to do was endure it! The whole service assumed that worship was something that someone else did to you, not something that you did together. Of course we are all meant to "bring" our own contribution to worship, but in effect there was little space for any of us to contribute anything. This brings us to the second point.

The whole service assumed that certain people had "authority" and that others did not. The sermon is a very good example of this. Here, one man stands in front of 200 other people telling them what the Bible says. The young people immediately found this alien. They wanted to have a say and who can blame them? After all, maybe 200 people thinking and discussing together might be more reliable than one person thinking on his or her own. What is for certain is that if everyone had a part in deciding what God was saying through the Bible that day, it would be more interesting! I'm not saying we totally abandon "preaching" or the idea that certain people have "authority", what I am saying is that we don't have to simply be spectators whilst someone else tells us what we should think. Everybody, and that includes young people, can give something to a church's life if they are given the space.

To be fair I have to say that most of the people who come to my local church are very happy with the services that happen there. They would deny that what was happening was "dull" or authoritarian. In fact, they find the services to be very life-giving and full of the Spirit. From their point of view they find the young people's criticisms very difficult to understand, let alone accept. So what we have here are two groups of people looking at each other across a divide. This divide needs to be looked at a bit more.

A matter of culture

Some might think the divide was simply the difference between those who are Christians and those who are not. In this case the explanation is obvious, the young people found the church service hard to handle because they had not yet become Christians. But this would be a mistake. I should point out that the young people that came to church that day were not at all against Jesus. In fact some were already praying, reading their Bibles, and calling themselves "Christians". That's why they were willing to give the church a try in the first place! But when they got there somehow they were not able to see in the services what the regular churchgoers see in them. The reason for this difference is a difference of culture.

The young people knew this right from the start. Their first reaction when they walked into the church was that they looked different to the other people there. Styles of dress relate directly to issues of "youth culture" as we have already seen. The same could be said of the music. What seemed very worshipful for the church folk, just made the young people laugh! Again we have seen that music is intimately a part of young people's "culture". When we come to the question of authority or sexism in the services the young people are again reacting out of their own cultural values and on that basis they found the church to be wanting.

Packaging Jesus

The divide between the young people and the church was caused by differences in culture. The young people were not rejecting Jesus, they were rejecting the cultural package the church had wrapped him up in. The music in church, the type of teaching, the styles of authority, these are all "cultural" factors within which the truth about Jesus is contained. They can therefore be seen as a kind of packaging or wrapping within which the Gospel is contained. For the type of people who go to church these things are very useful and helpful. They understand this type of "packaging" because it has evolved out of a culture which they understand. But the young people found this type of packaging did not help them at all. It came from a culture which they did not feel happy within. In fact, for some of them this culture represented many of the things they were reacting against when they formed their own youth culture. This is a very serious clash of interests at a cultural level which can cause problems for young people.

All change

Many young people faced with the culture of the church feel they must change if they are to fit in. This was certainly the experience of Kes, Charlie, and Chris, three working-class lads who became Christians. When they joined their local church they found that their lives changed in a number of different ways. Here they are talking together about these changes:

> Kes: "I don't know, the cost isn't so much material things. It's pride and self assurance, you know what I mean . . . People regarding you as soft and stupid . . . I know a lot of my brother's mates all blokes around fourteen and fifteen and that, regard me as stupid. I mean the way they talk to me and the way they look at me, they just think I'm stupid."
>
> Charlie: "Well I mean . . ."
>
> Kes: "No, but I mean straight up! and that hurts me because . . . well it just does you know. But it's pride. I mean as a Christian you lose your identity, don't you?"
>
> Chris: "But you find a new one, don't you?"
>
> Charlie: "Do you though?"
>
> Kes: "I don't know. I mean you have a notoriety to do something: 'Go away! Him! You know Charlie: fifteen pints a night and still drive home sober!' That sort of stuff. But after you're a Christian, they say 'Yeah, we used to see him down the pub now and again. Used to drink a bit' and in the end, 'Charlie? Oh him! He's a Bible puncher.'"[1]

We must not take lightly what Kes has to say. When he joined the Church certain changes were urged on him which had the effect of dividing him from his mates. His place in his community was so radically affected he began to no longer know exactly who he was and slowly his identity was being eroded away. Kes's testimony is very important because it raises the crucial question of identity.

Identity crisis

Youth culture is basically about identity. Whatever else is happening during adolescence the basic fact remains that young people are seeking to establish their place in the world. To do this they have chosen to form groups which have their own culture. All of the exciting variety and creativity we talked about earlier is aimed at one thing; making your mark on the world. The tragedy that Kes describes is the way that becoming a Christian has totally undermined this process and has replaced it with a way of life which alienates him from his family and friends.

We need to be clear here that it is not following Jesus as such which caused this alienation, but the cultural expectations the Church laid upon him. It is quite obvious that accepting Christ meant that Kes began to stop hanging out with his mates who went drinking. Kes took on this kind of behaviour because it was part of the "package" which surrounded Jesus. Accepting Jesus meant accepting this package and it was this that made his friends reject him. The atmosphere of the Church had produced a way of living out the Christian life which was based upon a middle-class culture which was largely unsympathetic to the kind of social life Kes was used to.

There must be some alternative to this destruction of a cultural identity. It can't be right that in choosing to follow Jesus young people have to cut themselves off from their own friends and families. The loss of identity and self-respect that went along with Kes's conversion seems to be the opposite of everything Jesus came to do. There must be a way of allowing Jesus to break out of the package we have put him in so that he can be re-packaged in a way which is more relevant to the culture of people like Kes.

Learning from the missionaries

What is really amazing is that the Church has actually faced these problems many times before in its history. Wherever the Church has grown as a result of "missionary" work people have had to wrestle with this issue of "culture". Take for instance the following situation described by an African Christian about his experience when his family came to follow Jesus:

"My own father's African name was Mangombe, meaning 'one who owns a large herd of cattle'. When he became a Christian, he was baptized Charles. My mother's name was Pfumai, meaning 'may thou be wealthy'. When she became a Christian, she was given the name Helen . . . In most cases names were chosen by the evangelist or missionary with no regard as to whether the family, for whom the name was initially significant of course, could even pronounce it at all."[2]

When the Church first started to evangelize in countries such as Africa, it was assumed that to be Christian you had to be "civilized". By "civilized" of course they meant Western and so whenever anyone became a Christian they were given a new, Western, name. This was a mistake which has led to so many horror stories about missionaries who expected African people to abandon their heritage and roots in favour of Western ways.

The frightening thing is that whilst the Church may now be aware of these kinds of problems around the world, we have not really learned these lessons here in Britain. Of course we don't give young people foreign names, but we do expect them to straighten out, and fit in with what we expect a Christian to look and act like. We don't very often say these things out loud, but whenever a young person lights up a cigarette, or swears, or talks about going "down the pub", we signal our disapproval. The mere fact that we as youth leaders feel uneasy about something can put pressure on individuals to try to be accepted and be acceptable to us. We might not realize exactly what we are doing when we pass comment on what seems like a fairly insignificant thing, but in fact we are starting to impose our "cultural" values on the young people. When we disapprove of a certain kind of music, or warn against going down to the disco, or make a joke about a curious hair style, we are rejecting the young people's culture in much the same way as the missionaries were rejecting their converts' African culture.

Learning the lesson

One of the most interesting features of our modern church life is that many African and Asian Christians are starting to find their own voice. In areas which were once places of "mission" there are now strong locally-led churches. These groups are talking about what it was like to be evangelized by the missionaries and they have an important lesson to teach us about culture and the Gospel.

The Asian writer C. S. Song tells a story[3] about a young newly-married girl. After the honeymoon she makes a meal for her husband and his four brothers. The brothers-in-law tell her they will only eat the meal she has prepared if she will tell them what their names are. The young girl says she does not know their names, so the brothers refuse the food. This situation goes on for quite some time, the girl cooks food that the brothers-in-law refuse to eat because she does not know their names. In fact, the only way she can break the log jam is by taking the time to learn their names from a small bird who sings to her every day.

C. S. Song likens this girl to Western missionaries who wanted to provide the people of Asia with "spiritual" food, but they were never willing to learn about the people they were trying to reach. By refusing to learn the names of her relatives this girl was in fact keeping herself separate from them: she was staying "single". Her brothers-in-law realized this and so wouldn't accept her food, which was a symbol of her acceptance into the family. This again was true of many of the Western missionaries, they wanted to share the Gospel but were not willing to step outside of their own cultural worldview to learn from other people. C. S. Song tells this story to point out why many Asians did not trust the Western missionaries and who in a sense can blame them? The Asian people realized that the missionaries were locked within their own cultural arrogance and it was this attitude which got in the way of spreading the Gospel.

What needs to be done

Christians in other parts of the world are all saying that the kind of cultural "imperialism" which went along with the Gospel when these countries were first evangelized was a big mistake.

If we are not going to simply repeat this mistake amongst young people in our own country then we need to take on board a new kind of approach to Christian youthwork. This new kind of approach has four special characteristics.

1. Adults meeting young people

Most Christian youthwork in this country has been based on the principle that "The best person to reach a teenager for Christ is another teenager". Whilst there is obviously a role for this kind of outreach we need to ask ourselves if young people, who are themselves going through the problems of adolescence, are really the ones best equipped to reach across cultural barriers. That most of our church youth groups contain one "type" of young person is no coincidence, "like attracts like". We need to accept the fact that Christian young people will be very able to share their faith with their friends, but their role needs to be supplemented with adults who can go to groups outside their present circle of friends. Crossing cultural frontiers is a very demanding challenge and it should not be left to our Christian young people.

2. Going to where they are

Most of our outreach has built into it the expectation that young people should come to us. We lay on evangelistic events in our church halls, or in Christian Unions or youth groups and we invite young people to come to us to hear about Jesus. We have got to reverse this approach – instead of expecting young people to come onto our territory to hear about Jesus, we must go to them. This means that Christian adults must commit themselves to going to territory where young people feel at home, be it the local park, shops, pubs or schools.

3. A change of attitude

When we go onto the young people's territory in the first place we need to go to learn. Young people have the right to expect that we know about their world, their language, their experience of life. They will ask us, just like the brothers-in-law in C. S. Song's story to "tell us our names". Facing up to this challenge is a very painful experience because there is much we will need to leave behind if we are going to be able to learn.

4. Starting with friendship

Sharing our faith across cultural frontiers will involve us in friendship with young people. As Christian adults we need to seek to form friendships based upon mutual respect. These friendships will take some time to form and they must not be a flash in the pan. Young people need to be able to trust us if they are ever going to trust in Jesus whom we follow. This kind of trust will be costly and can only be won on the basis of real friendship.

Doing what Jesus did

These four characteristics of youthwork are not really so strange. A short look at the Bible will show us that in doing these things we will actually be doing exactly the same thing Jesus did when he became a human being. Philippians puts it very neatly:

> The attitude you should have is the one that Christ Jesus had: He always had the nature of God, but he did not think that by force he should try to become equal with God. Instead of this, of his own free will he gave up all he had and took the nature of a servant. He became like man and appeared in human likeness. He was humble and walked the path of obedience all the way to death – the death on the cross. Philippians 2:6–8

It is a central theme in the Christian faith, that God, when he chose to communicate his message to us, took the form of a person. I suppose this seems pretty obvious, but it's a fact which often passes us by. God chose to become like one of us, because he wanted to communicate with us. This example should be at the heart of all our plans to reach out to young people. In doing this we are only doing what Jesus himself did, but if we are really following then there will be a cost. Meeting up with young people on their territory will mean having to "give up" certain things.

My own youthwork has followed this pattern for eight years now and I have to say that "giving things up" has not been easy. It has been very difficult at times to learn how to spend time with young people without having to be in control all the time. Running a youth group meeting or taking a Christian Union in a school is very challenging, but it has the advantage that you know you are in control.

It's quite another thing to walk up to a group who are having a smoke behind the school pavilion – the feeling is totally different. Instead of being an important person with a well-defined role you are a visitor on their territory, you have to obey their rules and accept the group as you find it. Instead of being the "expert" who has come to tell them about "the truth" you have to learn from them how to behave. It has been hard to leave my own comfort zone in an effort to get where young people feel at home. Listening to their conversation is an eye opener that has meant I see things very differently, and has also brought a new understanding. Going to their territory has meant that I know what their questions, concerns and bugbears really are. But what has been most challenging has been the realization that any authority or respect I have must come from the integrity of my life lived out amongst them. I can no longer rely on any position of superiority based on my age or my position as a youthworker. This is exactly what Jesus did when he became a man and lived amongst people in Palestine. In doing all of these things I am only trying to do what he did.

Friendship and the good news

It's this kind of friendship which is needed if we are to share the Good News about Jesus with young people. When we are so rooted in relationships with young people that their "names" are well known to us we will be in a position to demonstrate how Jesus makes sense in their lives and not just repeat how he makes sense in our own. But there is more to this than simply a neat way of communicating the message.

These kinds of relationships are themselves a part of the Good News about Jesus. When Jesus became a human being and formed friendships with his disciples he was demonstrating what it meant to be in relationship with God. To a lesser extent we are also called to be this kind of demonstration in the lives of young people. We do all of these things in the name of Jesus. We reach out as his body into the world extending his hands of love and concern when we form these kinds of friendships. In this way we are part of the Good News to these young people.

NOTES

1. Benington: *Culture, Class and Christian Beliefs*, pp. 23–24.
2. Song: 'Tell Us Our Names', p. 92.
3. Song: 'Tell Us Our Names', pp. 89–90

Picturing Jesus

Have you ever sat down and thought, "What does Jesus really mean to me?" It's a hard question to answer because Jesus is so special, and it's a challenge to put into words even one half of what he has done for us. One simple way that the New Testament tries to sum up what Jesus meant to people, was by giving him names. Some of these like "Son of Man" are used by Jesus about himself, others like the title "Lord" appear to have grown in popularity amongst the early Church. But wherever these names originated they are all an attempt to sum up the meaning of Jesus by drawing upon a particular idea or "picture".

Pictures of Jesus

One interesting "picture" of Jesus is found in John's gospel where Jesus refers to himself as "The Good Shepherd" (John 10:11-18). This "picture" must have been very powerful to the people who heard Jesus speaking, they knew all about sheep and shepherds and so the picture worked for them straight away. It was pretty easy for them to make the leap from actual shepherds they had met, to Jesus being a bit like these shepherds because he played the same sort of role in their lives: guiding, protecting and eventually giving up his life for the safety of us all. But this, of course, is not the only picture of Jesus that we see in the New Testament.

I have already mentioned the fact that very soon after the resurrection the early Christians began to refer to Jesus as "The Lord". In fact the phrase "Jesus is Lord" seems to have been one of the earliest confessions in the Church (1 Corinthians 12:3). Once again this title made incredible sense to these people who were used to talking about certain authorities, especially the Roman Emperor, as "Lord". By taking this kind of Royal title and applying it to the risen Jesus a kind of "picture" was formed which expressed the truth about Jesus. But putting these two ideas, Jesus as "Lord" and Jesus as "Shepherd", alongside each other raises a few questions.

In the first place, although both pictures come from the Bible they seem to express very different things about Jesus. The idea of a shepherd in the fields is a remarkable contrast to the idea of an emperor on a throne. It's hard to imagine an emperor having much to do with sheep, and it's even harder to see how a shepherd would want to rule an empire! But we have to admit both say important and true things about Jesus. The point here, surely, is that there are many ways of expressing the truth about Jesus. In fact the New Testament is full of "pictures of Jesus": Jesus the Priest, Jesus the Suffering Servant, Jesus the King, Jesus the Prophet, Jesus the Light, Jesus the Word, Jesus the Son. Each one of these "pictures" expresses the meaning of Jesus in an incredibly vivid way and this is part of the richness of the Christian faith, but it does beg the question – why so much variety?

Many pictures

We have touched briefly on the reasons for different ways of talking about Jesus already. One reason is that there were different parts of the Gospel message which needed to be expressed, so the resurrection and ascension of Jesus was better expressed by calling Jesus Lord. But there is more to it than just the unfolding of the Gospel story.

There is also the fact that within the New Testament we see the Christian faith as it moves from the Jewish world of Jesus and the disciples to the more "Greek"-thinking world of Paul and the churches he planted. Jesus the "Lord" not only expressed a Gospel truth, it expressed it well in the "Greek" culture of the rest of the world that Paul was evangelizing. To call Jesus "Lord" meant something to these people because they called people "Lord" in the everyday run of things. This of course can cause us some problems today when we try to use the same title for Jesus.

An everyday name of respect in the Roman world is not one we can use without some rethinking on our part. The title "Lord" for me usually conjures up an image of a wicked Norman knight in a Robin Hood story, or maybe a member of the House of Lords like Lord Longford. These pictures of what "Lord" means today cause a bit of confusion because I look at the Bible and Jesus doesn't seem to fit my picture of a Lord. Of course I experience the same sorts of things about Jesus as the early Church did, I see his reign in my life and I recognize his rule over the world. But this experience is not very well expressed by the word "Lord", because I don't use this word in the ordinary run of things.

These however are not very unusual problems. In Nigeria the missionary Charles Kraft found that differences in culture could quite easily result in misunderstanding.[1] On one occasion he was talking to a group of people and he said that Jesus was a shepherd. After chatting for a while he began to realize the group he was talking to were a bit confused about this picture of Jesus. On investigation Kraft realized that in their culture only mentally ill or educationally subnormal people were given the job of minding sheep. By calling Jesus a shepherd this missionary had given the people the impression that Jesus was a bit slow!

Any successful picture of Jesus will need to make sense in a culture. Charles Kraft discovered the hard way that his biblical study was not enough, he also had to be able to express the biblical ideas within the culture of the people that he was trying to reach. It was not enough simply to repeat a biblical "picture" of Jesus and hope the people he was talking to would understand. He had to be able to "translate" that biblical picture of Jesus into another culture. Sometimes this would involve finding another picture of Jesus from the Bible which made sense. But at other times he had to replace the biblical "picture" with a cultural equivalent of the people he was talking to. This idea of "translation" has been around for some time now in missionary circles but what is less well known is that we have already "translated" Jesus into our own culture.

Names and pictures

So far we have concentrated on the way a particular name or title is a kind of "picture" which carries certain meanings in our minds. But words are not the only pictures which tell of Jesus. Through the centuries Christians have tried to portray Jesus in art. In one sense there is no difference between these kinds of "pictures" and the use of various titles in the New Testament; each is trying to express the truth about Jesus in a relevant way for the time. These kinds of pictures are very interesting because they often have an extraordinary grip on our imaginations.

My wife, Tess, was given a Bible when she was a child; in it was a picture of Jesus coming out of the water after being baptized by John. Jesus in this picture has blond hair, blue eyes, and a white skin. In fact the very model of an Englishman abroad, he has even done his best to avoid the sun! Despite the semblance of Jewish costume that the artist has given to him, he is still unavoidably not Jewish at all in his looks. Talking with my wife about this picture, she was left with the firm conviction that this was exactly how Jesus actually looked.

It's fair to say that these kinds of pictures of Jesus are rare now, but that does not mean we have not invented modern day equivalents. In fact, there are a great many attempts to "picture" Jesus in ways that make sense to us today and who is to say that they will not be just as powerful in our imaginations?

Every picture tells a story

The other day I picked up a comic from my local Christian book store. It was the story of Jesus in pictures, just like any cartoon magazine. On the front cover we see Jesus, once again a white man. This blue-eyed and bearded figure is standing up in a boat commanding the waves to be still. His arms are strong and full of muscles, swinging around his neck is a red cloak and his disciples are looking on with amazement. Zap! Pow! – suddenly Jesus has become Superman!

Jesus as "Superman" is not as crass as it sounds, it is at least an attempt to express in our own culture, what and who Jesus is, by drawing parallels with a contemporary figure. However there is a serious problem here. Superman is a figure full of meaning already, and some of these meanings may not be good or helpful in the communication of the Gospel. So our attempts to make Jesus come alive within a culture by "picturing" him in new ways carry with them the problem that every picture has several meanings already.

This is an important point which needs to be understood and taken seriously. We need to recognize that any picture of Jesus, be it biblical or from contemporary culture, will be limited by meanings which already surround it. Of course it is right that we attempt to express the truth about Jesus within every age and culture. But we need to recognize that our attempts will need to be looked at in the light of the way that other people – particularly any groups we are reaching out to – see these pictures.

One problem here is that we are often fairly blind to the problems any one image of Jesus may have. Take for instance the picture of Jesus as a white man in my wife's old Bible. What in our country has seemed to be an OK picture of Jesus is fraught with problems. Take this Bible to Africa and give it to Black converts there and suddenly the whole issue of Christianity and Western domination rears its ugly head. By making Jesus into a white man we are saying that to be Christian you must be "Western". After all, how could you accept a white Western Jesus and still retain your own, African ways and culture? As we've seen, at one time most Christians saw nothing wrong with this kind of attitude, but now we realize this was a mistake which we need to sort out. One interesting point here is that it was the African people, whom the missionaries were reaching out to, who had to teach the missionaries which picture of Jesus made sense in their culture.

Similar problems emerge with the Superman picture of Jesus.

Some of us may identify with Superman, the outsider who comes to earth and fights injustice. The image of Superman has a good deal of power for us in our culture. After all, many films feature a powerful stranger as the hero, and a picture of Jesus in this style rings bells for us. The power of Superman for good has a lot of parallels with the life of Jesus. But in other ways this particular attempt at "picturing Jesus" has limitations. It's too "all American" for my taste, and the emphasis on the independence of Jesus and the force with which he makes his point is unattractive. Seen through the eyes of many women the violence and machismo of this picture of Jesus may make him unacceptable to them.

Problems with pictures

In many ancient churches, above the altar, there is often to be found a picture of Jesus. In what was called "the apse", which is a dome high at the front of the church, we see Jesus sitting on a throne with his right hand raised. His face is stern and painted all in gold, his clothes are regal and bedecked with many jewels and in his left hand he holds a book. This grand image of the risen Jesus reigning from on high became popular when the Church became accepted as the official religion of the Roman Empire. When Constantine became the first Christian emperor this new expression of the reign of Christ seemed to make a good deal of sense. The Peace of the Roman Empire (Pax Romana) merged in the minds of many Christians with the Peace of Christ.

For a while this picture of Jesus was very useful, but it meant the institution of the Empire was totally identified with the Christian faith. When the Empire went astray or when people were oppressed in the name of the Emperor, Christ was inevitably implicated. In later years the distant figure on the roof of the Church seemed to be too grand and remote, a person much more in tune with important and powerful people rather than with the poor or ordinary people. Those without power were alienated from Jesus by this picture. Of course, Jesus enthroned on high is a very biblical picture, but the cultural implications of making Jesus into a heavenly emperor got in the way of the truth of this image.

In other parts of the world Christians have also tried to escape old pictures of Jesus that were too much identified with the interests of the powerful. In Africa it is now very common for Jesus to be pictured as being black. This is a reaction to the "white" Jesus of the missionaries, but it does reflect the belief that Jesus is very much for the African people. A black Jesus is alive in Africa meeting people in their own culture.

Similar pictures are being made in South America. The Brazilian sculptor Guido Rocha has shown Jesus as one tortured on the cross. Guido was himself tortured and he has drawn upon this dreadful experience to say something about the cross of Christ. This Jesus is doubled up in pain, his ribs are bursting out of his body and he is screaming in agony and anger. This disturbing picture places Jesus in the same situation as all those who have been unjustly and insanely tormented. The message is clear: the suffering of Jesus means that God is no stranger to the sufferings of the Brazilian people. Jesus is one of them and on their side.

Looking through the eyes of young people

This has been a fairly long investigation of pictures of Jesus, but it has not meant to be simply an interesting "arty" exercise. Each of us needs to start to investigate our own, and our church's "picture" of Jesus.

One place to start is in the songs and choruses that we usually sing. It's worth taking an hour or so to look at the song book you use in church. I did this a while back and I was astonished to find that the chorus book we used every Sunday hardly ever talked about the earthly life of Jesus. In almost every song Jesus was pictured as the risen Lord on the throne of the people's praises. To be honest I found this to be a bit disturbing. My own picture of Jesus was as a friend who helped me through life; someone who had lived through all the things that I had gone through. Jesus on the throne seemed to be a bit immune from the trials and troubles of life and therefore was hard to relate to.

But there's more to this than interesting observations about Jesus. When we come to reach out to young people who are outside of the cultural framework of the Church we need to recognize that they may well reject our picture of Jesus. We need to realize that the kind of picture of Jesus which predominates in our church will almost certainly result from the way we see life from our perspective. When we start to get close to young people we might well begin to see that our way of expressing the truth about Jesus is as inappropriate as the picture of Jesus as white man in my wife's Bible. This does not mean we should abandon the Gospel, but that we need to realize that new pictures of Jesus will begin to be formed as we start to reach out to young people.

These new pictures of Jesus will come when we learn to look through the eyes of the young people we are reaching out to. In the first place this process will begin when we realize our own picture of Jesus does not work for these young people. For instance, Jesus as a King on a throne may not really make sense to young people having problems relating to authority. This is not to deny the fact that Jesus does have authority, the question is really how we communicate his special kind of authority.

Other biblical pictures of Jesus can be more helpful to young people, such as Jesus the prophet. Of course young people won't be familiar with the word "prophecy" today, but one of the traditional roles played by prophets in the Bible is that they called authority figures to account by often making very public protests. Jesus, too, protested in this way when he turned the tables over in the temple. Jesus as a protestor against injustice has a good deal of mileage to it.

Another biblical image of Jesus is as the person who will make space for young people and give them a position of respect above adults (Matthew 18:3, Mark 10:13–16).[2] Looking through the eyes of young people it is fairly easy to see that these pictures of Jesus might unlock the Christian faith to them in a way that always talking about Jesus as a nebulous "Spirit" on the throne might not.

Packaging, pictures and pain

In the last chapter I talked about packaging, and in this one I talked about "pictures". So it's probably fair to say at this point that in fact they are the same thing! Both are ways of looking at how "culture" has affected our perception and expression of what it means to be a Christian. I've spent some time on these areas because they are the key to reaching out to young people.

If Jesus is ever going to be allowed to come alive in the world of youth culture then we need to accept the fact that this will mean we will have to take Jesus out of the package. We will need to look through the eyes of young people to try to find new "pictures" of Jesus which carry meaning for them. This means we will have to learn to change and grow in our Christian faith as we get closer to young people. Eventually new ways of looking at Jesus will grow from a co-operation between adults and teenagers, each learning from the other. But in the first place the work has to be done by the adults – and this means change. Any kind of change is painful, it makes you feel insecure, unsure or just plain scared. But this is the kind of pain we will have to go through if we are going to follow the way of Jesus as he longs for us to reach out in love and friendship to young people.

NOTES

1. Kraft: *Christianity in Culture*, p. 14.
2. An idea suggested to me by Bob Dupee.

PART II

*

Altered Images

4

Getting to Know Young People

It's one thing "knowing about" young people, it's another thing actually to know them. "Knowing about" young people is relatively easy, reading books is a good way (including this one, of course), but if we really want to know a group of young people then it means we've got to start to get involved. There's no way around it, one way or another we've got to make a move. Personal contact is the only way to form a genuine friendship. But this is very hard and there are lots of things that make us adults very cautious about meeting young people. This chapter is a basic introduction to meeting young people for the first time, and in it I will try to give some practical advice to help soothe away some of the fears that we have when we think of meeting young people. This chapter will also give some ideas as to how and where to meet young people.

I feel scared

Everyone who works with young people at some time or another gets scared! Even the most experienced full-time youthworker feels a bit anxious about meeting a bunch of young people for the first time. So if you are getting cold feet, or wondering if you really are cut out for this kind of work because you are starting to sweat at the thought of meeting a strange group of young people, don't worry, it's natural – everyone feels that way at first!

It's probably a good idea at this point to have a brief word about full-time Christian youth leaders. Some people who work full-time with young people appear to be superhuman! They tell you impressive stories about how many times they did this or how many young people came to something or other.

When you've met them you are so impressed with their way with young people that you become convinced you are a worm incapable of doing anything! This is a big mistake – of course some people are gifted in their work with young people, but you don't have to be anyone special to form friendships with young people. "But . . ." I hear you say . . .

But don't I have to be young to do youthwork? No you don't, the best youthworker I know (and many of the young people I know agree), is a friend of mine from the USA. He is retired after a liftime working with young people. His experience is that teenagers want adult friends who have some kind of experience of life to share with them. Teenagers can talk to people their own age any time, but an adult is someone very special. My friend from the States is continually fascinated by young people and they in turn are very interested in him – especially because he is a grandfather!

But don't I have to be a bit more trendy? No you don't. In fact most young people will respect an adult more if they stick to their own styles and trends, however fuddy duddy! Trying to dress like a teenager when you are pushing thirty or even forty is a big no-no. Young people want to feel secure with the people they trust. It is very important therefore that we are reasonably comfortable with our own self-image. You don't have to apologize for being an adult – it's the one thing you've got going for you.

But don't I have to know all about their music? Again, no. Young people don't expect adults to know all about youth culture but they are very interested in anyone wanting to learn. When I was a teenager, next door there lived two old ladies who took a great deal of interest in me. One afternoon they sat through four sides of a record by the group "Humble Pie" – at the time they were a rather nasty heavy rock band. The old ladies must have hated every minute of it, but they were willing to listen to it with me because they cared about me. I was so chuffed that they were willing to at least give the music a try that I thought they were great!

But don't I have to be the sporty and active type? No – in being good at sport can be a disadvantage. Young people do not want someone who competes against them all the time, especially if the adult wins! It is always better if you are their supporter and fan, rather than the other way round. I find this all the time with rock music. I play in a band, but I don't want the young people to treat me as a hero, so I try to talk about their band's achievements as much as I can. You don't have to be good at something to be able to encourage someone else in their progress; anyone can be a fan!

Making contact

Starting a youthwork project is really tough when you don't know any young people. In fact most adults have very little contact with young people and this can be a very big barrier to overcome. How can you get to know people you never get to meet?

The answer of course is that if we want to get to know young people then we will have to go to where they usually hang out. This is a very hard thing to do, most of us are happier to stay with people we know and in places where we feel safe. Meeting new people is always a challenge, but speaking from experience I would like to say that it is not as bad as all that! Every year our students at Oxford Youth Works, who are training to be Christian youthworkers, have to go into our local schools to meet young people. They are always a bit nervous (or terrified) at visiting school for the first time as an adult, but they invariably come back having had a good time. More often than not relationships can be formed with young people in very easy and casual ways. Here are two stories which illustrate how two very different people got going:

1. Mary meets Sharon and her friends

Mary has just had a baby, it's her first. She lives with her husband, Mike, on an estate on the outskirts of her town. She's always had lots of friends through her work in the council offices, where she was very popular. She's also a member of the local Baptist Church, she left work when Andrew was born and has just started to lead a fellowship group for young mothers.

It's one of those glorious autumn afternoons and Mary has been down to the local shop to get something for tea. On her way back home she cuts through a small playing field where a group of boys is playing football. As it's such a nice day Mary decides to sit down on a bench, and that's when she met Sharon.

Sitting on the ground near the bench was a small group of girls smoking cigarettes and joking with each other about the boys playing football. One of the girls kept looking at Mary and at Andrew's pram, so Mary without thinking much about it said, "You can come and look at him if you want." Straight away the girl stubbed out her cigarette and came over to peer into Andrew's pram. "Cor, look at his smile, he's a real one this one is!" said the girl. "'Ere, have a look at 'im," she called to her friends. Before Mary knew it there was a group of girls getting together around the pram making admiring noises about Andrew. Mary didn't know quite what to do, she had to get back to make tea, so after a while she broke the party up.

When she got home the girl in the park kept coming back into Mary's thoughts and prayers. Two days later she was again on her way back from the shops when she saw the girls sitting by the bench as before. "Hi," Mary said sitting down on the bench and again the girls came round to look into the pram. "My name's Sharon," said the girl. "I'm Mary and he's called Andrew," she replied.

That was it really. I could tell you about the time Sharon and one of her friends came round to Mary's house or when Mary was rung up by Sharon late at night because her boyfriend had just given her the push, or even about the time when Sharon came on the church holiday to look after Andrew and the other children, but that would take too much time.

2. Tom plays Heavy Metal

It was late one Friday evening when Tom decided he needed to do something. For three years he had worked as a computer programmer and, true enough, he earned a fair bit of money, but he felt frustrated. Each week he would go to church and listen to talks about personal evangelism and being "on fire" for God, and then come Monday morning it was back to eight hours in front of the monitor and then three or four more in front of the telly at night. But next Monday was going to be different.

It was an advert in the local paper that set Tom off on this track. They needed help at the local youth club and he was going to give it a go. Tom realized he was not the most outgoing type of person, he didn't really have many friends, but something made him go for this advert anyway.

Judith, the youth group leader, was really glad to see Tom for she had been short of help for a couple of months now, but she also realized he needed to be slowly accepted by the youth group as he was not the attractive or easy-to-talk-to type. Judith asked Tom to spend most of the evening behind the coffee bar serving everyone that came in and after showing him the ropes she left him to it.

It felt really strange to Tom, but he relaxed when a young girl came up and asked for a Mars Bar – he obviously didn't look as strange and out of place as he felt! The next few weeks went by without much else happening; people came up and asked for things and Tom served them, it was all pretty straightforward really. But the next night everything changed.

When Tom got to the youth club there was a new bunch of lads standing around outside. They were a little bit older than the regular crowd and they all wore denim jackets with patches advertising bands on them. When the lads got inside they got hold of the tape recorder and sat around in the coffee bar playing the most ear-shattering noise Tom had ever heard. After about half-an-hour Judith came in and told them they had to move to another room, they were disturbing everyone else and it was unfair on Tom that he should have to put up with their Heavy Metal music. Tom saw the lads starting to get angry and so he said to Judith that he didn't mind the music at all. "Great!" said one of the lads, and he turned the din back on full blast!

The next week Tom was a bit disappointed that the lads weren't there when he arrived, but later on they sauntered in. "Hi Tom," said one of the lads, who was called Baz. Tom was chuffed, this was the first time in three months that any of the young people had recognized he was there, except to ask for something to eat or drink. It made him feel accepted by this group.

The next Saturday Tom was going into town, as usual, but this time he had decided to visit the local record shop. He wanted to know more about Heavy Metal, just so he could recognize a few of the bands.

Walking into the store he bumped into Baz and a couple of the lads. "Hi Tom, what you up to? Buying Barry Manilow's new one are you?" said Baz. A bit taken aback, Tom decided to admit what he was up to and see what happened. "Look, I don't know anything about Heavy Metal, could you give me some advice?" This seemed to do the trick. Baz looked so pleased that Tom was interested in his sort of music that he was soon pulling out records one after another and ranting on about how amazing this was and how incredible the other one was. Eventually with two albums under his arm Tom, Baz, and the rest left the shop.

Next week at the club Baz came in and demanded to know what Tom thought of the records. A lengthy discussion followed where Tom had to admit that he only really liked one of them, but he was willing to take some time to get into the other. At the end of the evening as Judith came in to lock up the lads pushed past her and yelled, "See you down the record shop on Saturday Tom," "Well, you've sure made an impact with them Tom, what's happened?" asked Judith. Tom told her all about it and was pleased when Judith encouraged him to keep meeting up with the lads. "They're a hard lot at first," she said, "but when you get through to them they have hearts of gold." One thing led to another and it wasn't long before Tom's

Heavy Metal record collection was pretty impressive, but the real breakthrough came when Tom had the lads round to his house to watch a video about Heavy Metal which he had taped off the telly.

Halfway through one of the songs Baz said how amazing the guitarist was. Tom, who had played a little guitar at school, said, "Yeah, it's hard to believe he's just playing two chords." The lads looked at him as if he was some kind of magician. "You mean you can play guitar?" one of them asked. Tom tried to play it down and say it was a long time ago and he hadn't kept it up and he only had an acoustic. But they didn't listen to him; they wanted Tom to show them how he could play the same chords as the Heavy Metal band were playing. So he reluctantly got out his old steel-string guitar, tuned it up and plonked out as best he could the two chords. "Show me how to do it," said Baz, so Tom passed him the guitar and Baz fumbled with his fingers until he could just make a noise. It was a magic moment and everyone there sensed it. "We could be a band!" they all seemed to chorus at once.

So that was how it started. With Tom two steps ahead of the rest of them they slowly began to learn to play the instruments Judith had managed to get for the youth club and eventually a band was born. One thing led to another, but it was only when they started to write some songs that the group first learned that Tom was a Christian. Sitting in his flat they were trying to think of some lyrics, when in desperation they turned to him for help. Tom said he was not very good at writing things but he felt it was important to sing about something that you really believed in. The discussion that followed produced the first song the band had ever written and it was all about the challenge of believing.

Learning from Mary and Tom

These two stories are typical of the way many young people are so open to adults – if they can only be given the chance to start being friends. Tom and Mary were of course very different; Mary was able to get into conversations very quickly, Tom was more withdrawn. But even in Tom's case when he put himself in the right situation and was patient he found the lads became approachable and even friendly. Both Mary and Tom took risks and they saw those risks as part of their Christian lives. It could be said that when they went out on a limb for God he honoured their risk-taking.

These stories show how we as adults can begin to take the steps which can open doors of friendship into the lives of young people. It's almost certainly true that in your own local area there will be young people like Sharon and Baz; it's just a case of finding out where they hang out and putting yourself in their way. Each of us is very different and we need to start by trying to sort out what kind of situation will best suit us. Not everyone can start up an easy conversation, like Mary did. It can be a lot harder for men to get into conversation so quickly. Judith was very wise; she realized Tom needed to be in a more structured setting if he was to feel comfortable enough to do his best. It's worth bearing this sort of thing in mind when you make your own plans to meet young people.

Getting down to it

Now and again in this book there are some exercises which are designed to help anyone who wants to start to form friendships with young people. The first one is a step-by-step guide which should help you if you are not sure where to start. The problem with guides is, of course, that some things they say are helpful and others are not. The same will be true of this one. It also needs to be said right at the outset that, unlike a travel guide, I have not been to meet your particular group of teenagers in your particular area. So be warned: this step-by-step approach needs to be used with some healthy caution and flexibility!

Exercise

STEP 1

Spend some time praying about what you are about to do. Bear in mind that setting out to meet this group (or groups) of teenagers is part of God's intention for his people. By reaching out in friendship you are joining in with the whole movement of God in our world. This means that time spent seeking God's face is always time well spent. Don't be afraid to ask God to reassure you, strengthen you, and above all go ahead of you. He knows these young people even if you don't as yet!

STEP 2

Over the period of time that you are praying begin to do some basic research in your local area. A good way to start is to sit down with a pen and a large piece of paper and try to figure out where young people naturally congregate. Do they hang around the shopping precinct at the weekend? Is there a particular place on one of the estates where young people just sit around? It could be in a park or outside the local chip shop or off-licence. Is there a sports hall where young people go, or some other kind of recreational facility? Do you know of any secular youth clubs or local sports teams which meet in your town? If you are free during the day you could think about local schools – do you know where these schools are? What do the young people do at lunchtime? Do you know what areas each school serves? In short try and get down on your piece of paper everything that you already know about your local area and the gathering places of young people.

STEP 3

The next thing to do is to try and check out what you have written down on your sheet of paper. Start going to these places and find out if what you have guessed are the habits of young people are actually true. It might help to keep some kind of written record as to what you have found out.

When you go to the local shopping arcade or the local estate or whatever it is, don't be afraid to spend a bit of time there. Make sure you appear to be relaxed in your manner. A good clue is to always try and sit down on a bench or lean against a wall, or whatever. If you stand and stare at young people you'll definitely freak them out! This is a good rule of thumb wherever you meet young people.

Whenever you come into contact with some young people try to make a mental note of as many details about them as you can – how are they dressed, what are they doing, how many of them are there?

If you find a particular group which interests you, make sure you go back to where you met them. It's worth trying to go to the same place at different times on different days just to see how often and how regularly this group can be found.

STEP 4

As time goes on and you continue to visit these places a pattern will begin to emerge. There will be a particular place or two where you have consistently met a group of young people. At the start of this exercise you have spent time praying that God will lead you to a group of young people, so don't be surprised if your thoughts continually bring you back to one place. This is the way that God often works!

STEP 5

Make a decision as to which group of young people you feel are right for you. Bear in mind your own gifts and abilities. If you are outgoing and happy to strike up conversations then a shopping precinct or a group that hangs around the local shops might be for you. If you feel the need for a more structured environment then a local sports team or a youth club might be more appropriate. One good guide is how comfortable you feel in these places and situations. More often than not a group will choose you by returning your friendship in some way.

Following these steps will get you started and by the time you get to Step 5 you will be well on the way to forming relationships with young people.

5

Building Up an Understanding

Most books on Christian youthwork start a chapter like this by quoting some ancient Greek who says how terrible the young people were in his day. Then they go on to talk about the 50s and how "teenagers" burst onto the scene with the films "Blackboard Jungle" and "Rock Around the Clock". Well, so has this chapter, in an off-hand sort of way! However, there is an important point here, for whilst it is true to say that the generation gap is not a new thing, the idea of the "teenager" in historical terms is relatively new. This, of course, begs the question "Why?" Why did people start to talk about teenagers as if they were something new and special?

Asking these sorts of questions is very important because it forces us to look for a better understanding of youth culture. In the last chapter I talked about practical ways we can get to meet young people, and this is obviously the place to start, but there are a lot of things which can help us as we reach out to young people. It is very useful to try to get a few handles on the reasons why we talk about adolescence as such an important time. One way to do this is to look at a few of the theories about young people which have been put foward. It probably should be said that this chapter is not by any stretch of the imagination an exhaustive or critical treatment of this subject. For those who want to pursue the material further the bibliography will provide a good starting point.

A period of transition

When teenagers first appeared in the 1950s sociologists tried to explain what was going on. In the USA a number of theories were thought up using the general sociological idea called "functionalism".

The main point about "functionalism" is that it argues that society is essentially like a biological organism, or a machine. All of the parts of society exist to make life work in the best way possible. From this viewpoint it was argued that "youth culture" came into being because it was "functional" for society, i.e: it was needed to make society work. Sociologists noted that growing up was particularly difficult in a modern society. Young people did not pass from being children to becoming adults immediately. In an industrial society there was need for a period of transition where young people learned the "skills" and responsibilities which came with adulthood. So between childhood and adulthood there are the years of education and training required by the advanced economies of the Western world if they are to have the right kind of work force.

The problem for young people is that they are effectively powerless during this transition period. They are on the margins of economic and political life and so have little or no say in what goes on. In response to this period of transition and powerlessness, sociologists said that young people formed their own groups and culture to help them through this difficult time. Young people form their culture, however, in the one area in which they can have some say – their leisure time. Whilst they are powerless in some areas of their life they can express themselves by choosing to dress in certain ways, or to listen to certain kinds of music, or to hang out in certain places. Youth culture then is the means by which young people over-come the "psychological" problems and tensions associated with the transition from being a child to becoming an adult.

From this point of view there is very little difference between a gang of skinheads and a university rugby club. Both "function" in the same way by banding young people together in groups where they can, at one and the same time, feel safe and begin to work out together what it means to be an adult. It doesn't matter that some youth cultures are shocking or offensive to adults, because they still enable young people to pass through a difficult time and therefore they are "functional" for the young people and also for society as a whole.

Using the theory: 1. Functionalism

Functionalism has much to offer to the youthworker. In the first place it seems to make a lot of sense to see the groups that young people form as a positive part of their growing up. If this is true then our role as youthworkers should be to build on the natural patterns that young people themselves have started to create.

It is a real temptation to see groups of young people as a "problem" needing to be solved. This is probably a mistake. Instead of trying to dissuade young people from their chosen social groups and behaviour we need to learn to co-operate with them. Young people are responding to the tensions they feel by making a group where they can feel safe. It is important that we can get alongside them in these groups and help them to grow through the experience of being a teenager.

Take the example of a gang of lads who hang out at the local shops. We might be concerned that they are involved in petty vandalism but we do not help them by trying to split up the group. It is perhaps a lot better to try to redirect the group's energy into a different kind of activity – maybe they could help to build a play area for children in the local park. Working with the group is always better than working against it.

This theory has also much to say about the youthwork that we set up. If young people form their groups in order to grow together into adulthood, then it has to be accepted that these groups will eventually break up. So any youthwork which plans to build on them will need to accept the fact that it has a limited life span. Young people grow up, indeed they must! If you succeed in getting your group to build a play area in the local park it has to be expected that individuals will slowly leave the group as they get jobs or girl/boyfriends and no longer need the security of the group. This has important implications where a group has started to explore the Christian faith. At first, the idea of faith and being a member of the group will be almost identical, but as time goes on and the young people get older there needs to be a growth in commitment to Christ which will be mature enough to survive without the group. Needless to say helping young people to develop this kind of faith is not easy!

A time for resistance

In the 1970s a group of sociologists in England began to write about what they called "youth subcultures". Their theories were based upon the idea that within a society there are differing cultural "ideas" and that these different "ideas" arise because of the basic economic structures that exist. Some people have power and some do not. They observed that most teenage groups in Britain came from the working classes and so instead of arguing like the functionalists – that all young people face the same basic problems i.e. growing up – they argued that working-class young people experienced a particular "working-class" way of growing up. They did less well at school, they left school as soon as possible, and experienced unemployment and the more "dead-end jobs". This experience gave form to a particular "subculture". These youth "sub-cultures" were a form of resistance to the influence of the dominant culture of the middle classes as expressed by all the major institutions like school, work, and, of course, the Church.

This group of sociologists talked about teenage "style" as a series of "rituals" which gave a "cultural space" where young people from the working classes could make some kind of protest. With this kind of perspective it could be said that when a group of young people wander down the street with a "ghetto blaster" blaring they are carrying their own "cultural" space with them as a protection against the rest of society. It should also be said that this kind of behaviour is also a form of protest because their cultural space is on display in such a public way.

Ideas about style were developed by this group so that they began to talk about the way that young people dressed as being "symbolic" of their rebellion. Style, they said, was a kind of guerilla warfare[1] which was full of rebellious meaning.

This general theory was developed later in a way which included "middle-class" rebellion by Mike Brake[2]. He argued that teenagers were essentially responding to "collectively experienced contradictions" in society's structure. In this way the phenomenon of middle-class "hippie-type" groups could also be seen as a response to the way middle-class young people experience society. Brake's general approach does to some extent combine elements of the functionalist theory because of the stress on the problems young people face. But at the same time it does allow for the element of "class" which is so important in a British context.

Using the theory: 2. Resistance

If youth subcultures are actually a comment on the tensions and contradictions which young people experience as they grow up then they deserve to be taken seriously. From a youthwork perspective it is not at all satisfactory to simply "humour" young people in the cultures they adopt. It is perhaps more valuable to try to understand what the meaning of any particular "style" actually is. Articulating this meaning in a positive atmosphere with young people can be very fruitful.

If we take the example of our group of lads who hang around the local shopping precinct we could perhaps see that their use of graffiti may actually be an attempt to make their mark on the world. There may be specific grievances or issues which have stirred them. As a friend and a youthworker it may be possible to find other, more constructive, ways of helping them to get their message across.

Rebellion and conformity is crucially important when we come to try and share faith with young people. We need to be aware that many young people are adopting styles which indicate a set of values protesting against institutions like the Church. If we are to take the culture of young people seriously then this means that we need to recognize that many of their criticisms of the Church are important and in some cases valid. When these young people begin to "picture" Jesus from their own perspective what will emerge will be threatening to "traditional" values in the Church. (This theme is explored more deeply in the last part of this book.)

There is also in this theory about youth culture a stress on the different groups that there are amongst young people. It is important to recognize that in any one town there may well be three or four different youth subcultures. This variety is very important because it shows how groups of young people from different social backgrounds respond to the experience of growing up.

When we come to try to picture Jesus for one group of young people we need to recognize the relationship which exists between the different youth subcultures. In the long run, Christian mission in our society needs to lead to not just individual change at the personal level, but change at the social level. Youth subcultures provide us with vital clues as to how we can approach this complex problem by giving us a more "corporate" picture of society.

Reading the patterns

Reading a history of youth subcultures in Britain can be a bit confusing. Knowing about Teddy Boys or Skinheads or Punks may be very interesting, but these groups are not always part of our particular youth scene (and even if they are they sometimes have changed radically from their original form). One way around this problem is to develop a basic pattern or framework which any groups you come into contact with can be fitted into.

It is fairly safe to say that youth subcultures basically follow the patterns of social organization which already exist in our society. Working-class young people basically form "working-class" youth subcultures and middle-class young people form "middle-class" subcultures. As the relationships between the classes in our society change then youth subcultures have followed suit. Thus in the 80s with the growth in the middle classes there has evolved a much greater variety of youth subcultures amongst middle-class young people.

So the basic divisions in our society could form the vertical lines of our pattern: Working Class, Middle Class, Upper Middle Class (see figure 1). To these verticals there should be added horizontal lines labelled, Straight, Mainstream and Rebellious.

Working Class	*Middle Class*	*Upper Middle Class*
Straight	Straight	Straight
Mainstream	Mainstream	Mainstream
Rebellious	Rebellious	Rebellious

FIGURE 1

Using this basic pattern it is possible to begin to plot youth subcultures. In doing this it must be stressed however that many youth subcultures will hang untidily from one of the squares formed into its next-door neighbour. It also needs to be said that over a period of time as youth cultures change and develop different groups will influence and affect each other. In the next section I will describe a number of youth subcultures which were around Oxford in the mid-80s and plot them on this pattern (see figure 2) to show their interrelationship.

Casual

The mid-80s place us in the middle of the Thatcher years. In the south it became a matter of belief that given a little hard work anyone could make good. The prize was there for anyone to grab if they wished. At this time working-class young people increasingly began to dress in ways that echoed some of the most treasured status symbols of the upper classes – dark blue blazers with badges announcing membership of a polo club; ties which closely resembled those that tell membership of an exclusive public school Old Boys club. In fact almost everything these young people chose to buy from the shops was encrusted with one or other kind of ensignia from the rich – and upper – classes.

Of course in reality very few, if any, of these young people had ever been skiing in Aspen, Colorado, or had a clue what the rules of polo actually were. And if you asked them what they expected to do with their lives, usually they would say they would work in the factory like their Dad. Mike Brake argues that young people create subcultures to resolve "contradictions" in society. For these working-class young people there is the contradiction that they are told by the media on the one hand that they can make it if they work, and on the other there is the testimony of their parents and their older brothers and sisters that there is not really any escape from their local area.

Style amongst rebellious working-class young people at this time was simply an exaggeration of this way of dressing – however it was combined with a lifestyle of minor violence and petty crime. In Oxford this usually took the form of "Froggy bashing", a favourite pastime amongst many working-class lads who took to going into the centre of the city to pick fights with the foreign language students who proliferate in the summer. Added to this was the habit of taking cars and going joy-riding.

Rasta

For black teenagers in Oxford in the 1980's there was a basic split between those who simply went along with the mainstream style adopted by working-class casuals and those who follow a more "Rasta" style. The Rastafarian religion was started by Marcus Garvey in the West Indies and had spread to Britain by the 1970's. In the mid-80's reggae music was still very influential with young people starting to "Toast" over the top of reggae tracks played through massive "sound systems". Toasting was a kind of improvised poetic chant, much like rap, but more West Indian than American. Rasta style at this time involved growing large bundles of dreadlocks, often kept in place by a large woolen cap which bounced up and down as you walked along.

More often than not these young people would wear a track suit made from a slinky material. Along with this style often went a habit of smoking marijuana (ganja). Curiously, whilst the hair style and the music point to a yearning to get back to their roots, a longing for Ethiopia which expressed a sense of Africanism for many young people, the track suit points toward the usual stereotype of the athletic black sporting star. Incidentally, Bob Marley was crazy about football, he played every day. Rasta-influenced young people were in many ways lodging a protest about the kinds of lives they were living in Britain. But the track suit might point to the fact that sport is one of the few ways a black young person could make it in British society.

Sloan

This girl comes from the more prosperous side of our town. In the mid-80's she and her middle-class family are in many ways the real winners. They have had it very good and have been told not to be ashamed of their good fortune, because eventually everyone will begin to feel the effects of prosperity. Wealth will inevitably "trickle down" and reach even the poorest in society.

Draped around this girl's shoulder is a very expensive sweater; she's got a number of them just like it. But this valuable item is not treated with much respect. By hanging it around her shoulders she has firstly told us she has enough money to treat this jumper with disdain. But she has also raised the jumper up to some height so we can all see what she has done. The striped trousers are almost as loud as this girl and her friends when they get a few drinks inside them in the local wine bar. Why be quiet when she has everything going for her?

But on the other side things aren't so comfortable. Twenty years ago this girl's parents could be fairly certain of a place at university and after that a job in a respectable profession. These were reasonable expectations simply because of the fact that they were born into an upper-middle-class family. But now this girl cannot be so confident, she has to make her grades at A-level and when she leaves university has to compete against the new up-and-coming "yuppies". Her style reflects this essential contradiction in her experience of the mid-1980s.

Goth

The Sloane and the Casual have bought into the bright new world that is dawning in Mrs Thatcher's Britain, but this is certainly not true of the Goth. The style is certainly fairly shocking when you first meet it – it's somehow reminiscent of late-night horror movies. The word "Gothic" originated with the 18th-century school of sensationalist romantic literature, those Gothic horror stories, perhaps best captured in the works of Edgar Allan Poe, Mary Shelley and Bram Stoker. With the white face, black make-up and hair the Goth look has come straight out of a Hammer horror movie. This is one of the living dead, a vampire.

Symbols abound with the Goth. Crosses tell us of more mystical than material values, just as the Indian skirt similarly points us towards an alternative approach to life. This is a hippy but of a much darker and cynical kind. What is interesting is that this young woman is most probably very talented. She will come from a home not too dissimilar from the Sloane pictured above. She may well still be in higher education, but on a cultural level her message is very clear; she has turned her back on Thatcher's "success"-related dreams. Instead, for her, life has become a living hell filled with death, and instead of material advancement she seeks a more "mystical" path.

Punk

Punk style was still very much alive in Oxford in the mid-80s but it was exclusively adopted by homeless young people who congregated in the centre of town. Oxford has a very large number of homeless young people. Punk expressed their feeling of total alienation. Shaved heads served to shock and send a strident message which tells of a person washed up and out of the rat race.

Glue sniffing was just another way of getting out of it and into a self-destructive haze. At this time to hang around in the park with a plastic bag full of glue was only ever a last resort for very desperate young people. For some this public show of being at the bottom of the pile became an important way to shock those of us with whom they shared the streets during the day. Curiously enough, as well as begging on the street some of the more colourful punks would charge tourists wanting to take their photograph!

Straight

There are always a small group of mainly middle-class young people who play no part in the general flow of youth subcultures. I have labelled these straights, mainly because they simply follow the styles of their parents. These young people were more often than not very academic and destined for a successful university career. Perhaps to express where they are headed they identify with forty-year-olds in their choice of clothes.

Working Class	*Middle Class*	*Upper Middle Class*
Straight	Straight	Straight
Casuals Mainstream	Mainstream	Sloane Mainstream
Punk Rebellious	Rasta Heavy Metal	Goth Rebellious	Rebellious

Understanding the signs and symbols

From this quick snapshot of young people in the mid-80's we can see some of the variety of styles that are adopted at any one particular time. In attempting to get behind the images I have had to be very subjective in my interpretation. It's hard to say to what extent these readings are correct. The picture gets even more confused when we talk to the young people themselves because they will often have no idea about these kinds of theories! This in itself should urge us to caution. In the final analysis each young person is an individual and should be treated as such.

Exercise

Reading the styles of different youth subcultures is a very complex business. This exercise aims to help in approaching this type of analysis but essentially it involves having an imaginative eye on three different areas – mainstream culture, Pop culture and the style of young people in your area.

1. *Mainstream Culture*

Take a piece of paper and begin to "brainstorm" as many factors currently likely to affect young people – for example, changes on the political scene, changes in current popular opinion, changes in education.

Keep an eye on the Sunday supplements and other opinion-forming magazines like *New Society* or *Cosmopolitan*. Try and form a few impressions of the main changes happening in the cultural life of our society.

2. *Pop Culture*

It's worth taking, for a while, a number of the different music magazines and newspapers. Reading this stuff can be a bit bewildering, they seem to talk about bands and people you've never heard of. But over a period of time a few impressions will begin to form which can give helpful indicators as to the kind of issues which concern young people. It's worth finding out about the kind of things some of the bands are singing about. *Top of the Pops* represents the mainstream of music consumed by young people, but if you want a more complete picture then you need to get hold of some of the music in the independent record charts.

Once again brainstorming can be a good way of getting down on paper what you have learned from your research. When you have a good amount of material down on paper you can then begin to find patterns and relationships between everything that you have written.

3. Subcultural Style

From your own research (Chapter 4) you should already have a good idea of the kinds of style you have in your local area. It's worth trying to get to grips with particular symbols and ways that young people choose to dress. You may find there is one item of clothing that most young people in one of the groups you have met wear. Spend some time thinking about this item of clothing. Could it have any significance as a sign? Have these young people adopted this item of clothing from somewhere outside of their own cultural environment? Does this item of clothing have any other function or meaning outside of its use by these young people?

To get anywhere in this kind of analysis demands that we try to bring together general culture, pop culture and teenage styles of dress. But it's also looking at the way a particular group talks. Style in language can give similar clues to those we find in dress. The "rap" music which has its roots in black American culture has its own ways of speaking. Some young people have adopted aspects of this language as their own. Here, movement in popular music has been seen as relevant to young people today.

Can you detect similar developments in your area and young people? Are there any reasons which you can think of why these young people may choose to adopt a particular style of speaking?

NOTES

1. Hebdige: *Subculture: The Meaning of Style.*
2. Brake: *Comparative Youth Culture.*

6

Friendship

Friends are the most important people to teenagers. A friend is someone to share secrets with, someone to go out with, someone who listens, someone who thinks you're all right, someone you can trust. We all want friends, we all need friends, but to a teenager they are what life is all about and they are very special. Suddenly, for the very first time, you have some freedom from your home and your parents, and you find this freedom amongst your friends. Going out with your mates brings you into a whole new world full of exciting and dangerous things to get up to. This is a world which is all of your own making, a world your parents have no idea about.

But does every young person *really* feel this way about their friends? Could it be that different kinds of young people experience different kinds of relationships with their friends?

Patterns of friendship

Friendship amongst young people is a very varied thing indeed, but it is possible to begin to discover patterns of friendship. Young people from different subcultures relate to each other in quite remarkably different ways. The following descriptions are based upon my own observations and upon the experiences of several young people I have known. Of course this chapter is not the last word on this subject; I have not followed any scientific method here, but these impressions of friendship amongst young people may give a few landmarks and points of contrast for your own research.

1. Outside the chippy

On the estates around Oxford young people can often be found loitering on the streets. More often than not a particular place becomes a meeting point. It could be outside the local shops, under a particular lamp post, by the children's swings in the park or even outside the chip shop. In one rural village I heard of a group of young people who colonized the bus shelter. These groups are usually made up of boys, although some girls will share in some of the activities, and they number from eight to twenty-five, with membership always being a bit fluid.

The young people who get together in these places will nearly always live locally. In fact, the estate will be of primary importance to them. Sometimes groups can form a very close identity with a special name and even a special language. A couple of years ago a group used to hang out in one of our local parks who called themselves "The Florence Park Posse". They even had their own whooping cry – a kind of secret signal which they used whenever they wanted to call together their gang.

Friendship amongst these groups is based on the fact that they all live in the same area and that they join together in shared activities. Just hanging around outside a chip shop might not seem to be much of an activity, but this is often the jumping-off point from which something else happens. More often than not the group will be simply waiting for something to turn up, or for someone to have an idea. It might be that a stranger comes along whom they can poke fun at, or that someone has a moped they can ride around the local park.

Being accepted as part of one of these groups can involve a certain amount of testing. If the group has taken to fighting with a neighbouring group of young people, or is involved in some kind of petty crime, then new members are expected to show a certain amount of daring. There is also a very strong expectation of loyalty. "Grassing" another member of the group is considered to be the worst offence and will be punished by a severe beating, although in practice very few members will tell on their friends. "See everything, say nothing" is a saying which is stuck to very fiercely.

These kinds of groups are not a safe environment in which problems can be discussed. If a serious problem – like the fact that someone might be going to be in trouble with the police – is brought up, more often than not it will be joked about. Personal problems or feelings are never talked about in any depth at all for the emphasis is upon having fun. There is also a marked intolerance of anyone who doesn't fit. People are judged immediately upon the type of clothes they wear and the colour of their skin. Foreigners, either from ethnic minorities or in terms of class, are objects of ridicule and sometimes attack. In Oxford there is a good deal of tension between groups of Asian young people and these working-class groups. There is also a good deal of feeling against "students" which sometimes spills over into violence. This tendency is always increased if the foreigner or student is seen to be invading the group's territory. Even within the group it is possible for one person to always be picked on by the others. In one group I heard of a lad who lived on the local caravan site and who was always the butt of any joke because he was a "Gypsy".

As young people grow through the various stages of adolescence their relationship to the group will change. At first the average 12, 13, 14-year-old will be on the fringes of the group. Within their age group they will probably spend more time playing football, but they will hang around with the main bunch from time to time. From age 14 to 16 they will be right in the heart of the group trying either to be the most daring or the most funny. As soon as they can look old enough to get served, they will graduate into the pubs. Some will head for the centre of town and the night clubs, whilst others will get more heavily into thieving, especially of cars. Others will quieten down a bit and go steady with a girlfriend or start to hang out with one or two closer friends.

2. Girls talk

It is a general rule that girls talk to each other much more than boys do. There is in most adolescents a progression towards more intimacy as they get older but this is particularly true of girls. One study divides adolescence into early, middle, and late periods[1]. In the early years (11–13) friendship is more often than not centred around activities like playing or dancing classes. In the middle period (14–16) more intense friendships are formed which often focus around a sense of security, and friends fall out because someone told someone what someone else didn't want them to know! In later adolescence (17–20) friendship is a bit more mutual and relaxed. Going out with a boyfriend is not seen as so much of a threat to the relationship any more. The ability of girls to talk to each other and share troubles is seen in both working-class and middle-class groups.

One group of girls, aged between 14 and 16, which I was told about used to meet sitting on a wall around the back of the school. All eight of them lived on one of the estates near the school. Unlike the lads outside the chippy these girls would be constantly talking to each other about a wide variety of subjects – in particular the sharing of information, wisdom, and ignorance about sexual matters. Weaknesses, and a sense of hurt, were all readily acknowledged, but there was also a strong sense of what was right and what was wrong. Thorny problems like how to make your mum let you go out when she said you couldn't, or whether a guy should wear a condom, were discussed to sort out the "right" answer.

Sharing amongst a group of girls can involve very close relationships between two or three girls, even though they are also part of a group. One "threesome" of middle-class "rebellious" girls I knew were always having deep conversations with each other. The friends would meet at each others' houses, sometimes staying overnight. At 14 they looked old enough to go "down the pub" and every Saturday night along with a group of 10 or 15 girls large quantities of Malibu were consumed! But when it was all over the smaller group would stay overnight with each other.

In this group very intimate things were shared as a matter of course. Struggles with parents were a constant issue to be worked through, since most of these girls had significant stress in their home lives. Struggles with school were another important ingredient where minor victories or injustices were chewed over in a supporting environment. There was an extraordinary sense of closeness between these girls – one couple I knew told me they often had times when they shared the same thoughts at the same time, even though they were in different places.

Some girls will express their closeness by almost magical expressions of bonding like cutting themselves in the same place or making vows to keep faithful to each other. Needless to say, however, there were some tensions between different members of the threesome, for in any triangle there will be some problems associated with favouritism. What was interesting was that alliances changed as other factors, like a new boyfriend, altered the pattern for a while.

3. Down town

Friendship patterns between young people can be based simply on the way that people dress. There was a group of young people in Oxford who called themselves "Alternatives". Their style of dress was largely individual but it was an extension of "Gothic" style where hair would be crimped or shaved or formed into dreadlocks. Clothes would involve a number of different layers and combinations of jackets and coats. These young people were normally middle-class and fairly intelligent, their parents were usually slightly alternative themselves, and therefore more tolerant of their teenagers' taste in clothes.

These young people found each other by hanging out in a particular place in town. At certain times, like 4 pm after school or around 2 pm on a Saturday individuals would head down to the meeting place in town – although there was never any guarantee that anyone they knew would actually show up that day. That was not the point, because these young people were interested in meeting new people. From these informal contacts friendship groups would be formed which drew young people from every part of the city.

Mutual acceptance was an important feature of these groups. Talking with a working-class lad who used to hang out with his mates on the estate and occasionally met up with one of these more "alternative" groups, he was very sure that people were accepted by the middle-class group much more easily. His own experience was that even though he did not dress like an Alternative, he was given the space and the time to form friendships all the same. People were judged for who they were, not by what they wore or where they lived.

Trust was expressed in very concrete terms by the Alternatives. Clothes would be shared and almost held in common. On one occasion I knew of a leather jacket (a prized and pricey item) which was lent to an individual for over five months!

Sharing also took place at a personal level – problems were there to be shared but in a fun environment. One habit that was widespread for a while was called "The truth game". This involved a group of young people agreeing with each other that they would answer whatever question they were asked by one of the other group members. Furthermore, any answer given was a secret which could not be disclosed. Although I was in close contact with this group and often told how "wicked" a certain question was and who asked it of whom, I was never told what the answer was!

4. I'll give you a ring

So far I have only discussed groups that could be considered to be a bit "rebellious", but mainstream middle-class young people also have a very interesting pattern of relationships.

In one group of young people the phone was the most important feature of contact. Activities were planned ahead of time so that everyone knew what was going to happen. Someone would ring up another member of the group and arrange to meet, perhaps at a pub. Maybe there was an event which was being organized, like a party at someone's house, or a barbecue at the local football club. Word would spread informally around the group in such a way that everyone knew where they were going to get together that night. This kind of organization is in marked contrast to the more informal contacts which we see in groups 1, 2 and 3. There is an element of control and achievement about the group which gives a real sense of security, but there is not the same identification with an area or a strong sense of style.

This kind of group will start from around the age of 16, but its key members are a little older. Usually the friendship network will include boys and girls with a mix of older brothers and younger sisters. In some cases the wider group can rise to about 30 young people who get together for some event or other. Talking is very important to the group, they will choose pubs which are quiet and comfortable to chat in, but the emphasis will be primarily on having fun. Eventually the members will all go off to college or get jobs and move away. The informal relationships based around the phone will keep some contact going even in this more fluid situation, but the group as such inevitably has to come to an end.

Following the pattern

Each group of young people will have its own ways of organizing its friendship patterns. These four examples provide some insight into the ways young people who are part of different social groups and youth subcultures relate in different ways. It is important to recognize that the context within which friendship is experienced by young people may be very different.

The fact that ways of relating and communicating with each other may be so varied has a number of implications for any adult wishing to form friendships with young people. In the first place it makes a lot of sense to try to learn the rules of any group you come into contact with. My own experience of meeting up with young people is that a good deal of frustration comes from unrealistic expectations of friendship. Whilst I might want to spend time talking at a deep level about feelings and issues, the group I'm in contact with may ordinarily only want to do things together. All my attempts to start a conversation may fall flat because I have not learnt the rules of communication which the group ordinarily follows. Getting this sort of thing right takes some time and patience, just as learning another language takes time.

Friendship patterns are also very important when any strategy for youthwork is being planned. It makes no sense to contact a group who meet outside a shop on an estate with the intention of getting them to come to a youth club or church on the other side of town! Similarly it would make very little sense to start a work amongst working-class boys which is based around discussion and sharing, when all they want to do is play football.

The patterns described in this chapter may well be typical; however there will be many others which you will come across in your area. But whatever the pattern, it is very important that we are able to respond to the kinds of friendship the young people themselves are most comfortable with. Fighting an established pattern is at best a waste of time and at worst cultural arrogance. People are very different and varied and we need to accept this fact.

The real question is: how can Jesus become part of this friendship pattern in a natural and yet a challenging way? We should not be seeking to simply substitute one pattern of relating for another. Rather we need to be seeking to be part of the process by which Jesus enters the friendship pattern of a particular group and renews it from within.

NOTES

1. Douvan and Adelson in Coleman: *Relationships in Adolescence*.

7

Music

Bill Haley, of "Rock Around the Clock" fame, is reputed to be the one who started it all. Suddenly in the 50s young people latched on to Rock and Roll and the teenager was born. Since that time youth culture and popular music have always been closely related. This relationship is very complicated, for not only have musical styles changed over the years, but so has the way young people choose to use music. So, to understand the meaning of any particular song it is not enough simply to listen to the lyrics on the record, it is also necessary to look at how young people use it.

Marvin Gaye's "I Heard It Through the Grapevine" is a good case in point. In the 60s the Motown Sound grew out of the working-class, black culture of motor city, Detroit, Michigan. But very soon middle-class teenagers in America picked up on this music and made it their own. In the 1970s, however, working-class Skinheads in Britain could be seen dancing to Marvin's dulcet tones. In the 80s middle-class American advertisers revived their favourite hits from the 60s to sell jeans or to use as soundtracks to films. A new generation of middle-class young people listened to "I Heard It Through the Grapevine". In each of these situations the record was the same, but its meaning changed as each group invested it with new associations, images, and emotions.

Teenagers are far from being just passive consumers of music. In fact there is a constant dialogue between popular music and youth culture, each affecting the other. This chapter will explore the ways different groups of young people interact with different musical styles in the hope that this will shed some light on what is a very intimate part of most teenagers' lives.

Heavy Metal thunder

Heavy Metal is probably our most enduring youth subculture. Starting in the early 1970s it seems that somewhere or other there has always been young people who identify with this kind of music. What is particularly curious is that these young people, unlike most other youth subcultures, have always been defined by the music they listen to. This is reflected in their lack of a real name – at times they have been called Metallers, or Metal Heads, or Metal Freaks, or Hairies, but none of these names has really stuck. This is despite the fact that in terms of style they have a very distinctive image. Typically this would include skin-tight denim jeans, baseball boots/trainers, tight tee-shirt or vest and a denim jacket with a large patch on the back advertising a Heavy Metal band.

For the uninitiated, Heavy Metal is basically about noise and power, or rather it is about male power and noise. From start to finish a Heavy Metal concert or video is a celebration of male sexuality and fantasy. Guitars become phallic symbols caressed in a sexual embrace, scantily-clad women are paraded in front of the all-male band, and everything is shrouded in a sound which rivals the noise created by a jumbo jet taking off. There's no doubt about it; Heavy Metal has managed to create a world where anyone with a guitar and a large enough amplifier can be a real powerful man.

It's probably no surprise that most Heavy Metal fans are young boys, although this is by no means exclusively the case. This kind of music is ideal as a way of asserting their identity as men, although this identity is one which is often far from reality. Most young Heavy Metal fans are from lower-middle-class families, and usually it has recently made the shift from the working class to a more middle-class way of life. The success of the family in this respect will involve a fair amount of dislocation for the young person. He feels out of place with the lads on the estate, because his family has just bought their own home. Anyway, it is likely that his parents insist he stays in. Instead, there is a fair amount of pressure to succeed at school, to get on in life like his parents have. Heavy Metal is one way to resolve this sense of powerlessness and lack of identity.

When you listen to Heavy Metal at the right volume (louder than you can stand) you get a buzz. The sheer noise, particularly the way the music emphasizes bass notes and gritty rumbling distortion, makes you feel ten feet tall. I remember one young person saying to me that when he listened to Heavy Metal was when he felt most alive. In some ways I don't blame him, taking GCSEs is no fun, and everyone is allowed a certain amount of escape. This in simple terms is what Heavy Metal is about – it is an escape into a world where young people can feel they have control, that they can make their marks in life, and can at last lose their virginity! This will be a place where women will not order you to be in by a certain time, where status can be earned with a simple twiddle on the guitar and where boys can be as naughty as they want to be.

Heavy Metal and Christians

Christian commentators have never really come to terms with Heavy Metal. One of the problems is that in the past some Heavy Metal bands have used occult symbols and sung songs about the Devil and Satan – in fact the very first Heavy Metal band was called "Black Sabbath". I can't help thinking that Christians have been spooked by this sort of thing and have failed to look at the real issues which lie behind this kind of music.

The meaning of Heavy Metal is not in the lyrics of songs, it is in the heads of all of those bedroom-bound rockers. The occult image is just another easy way to feel powerful and appear bad to everyone. In dealing with young people who are into Heavy Metal we need to take this issue of power and identity very seriously. Whilst any occult influence is very unhealthy we need to realize that most Heavy Metal fans are just trying to shock and appear to be something they are not. In most cases the occult image was just a sham. In the 80s one band with an occult reputation was called Demon. Chatting with their bass player he admitted to me that it was all just a ruse to sell records. This is, of course, a fairly cynical approach to young people, especially if some are tempted to experiment with occult matters. But before we condemn these bands too readily we need to take on board the cause of this subcultural style amongst young people.

These young people are reacting to the stresses and strains our adult world places on them. The ironic thing is that many of the values currently in our churches are exactly the kinds of values that create the atmosphere where young people feel the need to get into Heavy Metal. In the Church we want people to get on in life, we try to encourage young people to study, and in some cases membership of a church may be the cause of a family being upwardly mobile. Perhaps this is why we get so worked up about Heavy Metal – these young people are directing their rebellion against us!

Play that funky music white boy

Rock and Roll was created out of a mixture of blues, gospel and country music. White musicians heard the rhythms and singing style of black people, combined these influences with their own music and took the world by storm. The history of modern pop music is full of examples where music which originated in the black community is taken up and popularized by white musicians. This fact has meant that popular music has become a place of dialogue and conflict where black and white young people are in constant communication. Reggae music, which originated in the West Indies, is an interesting example of this.

Reggae has been very closely connected with Rastafarianism which is a mixture of Christian belief and traditional African religion. In short Rastas were protesting against the influence of the white man on their lives. This was summed up in the phrase Babylon. When Reggae came to Britain in the seventies-early-eighties it struck a chord with many disaffected black young people. Unemployment, racism, and poverty were rife, and in this context Reggae, with its message of a homeland in Ethiopia and freedom from the bondage of Babylon, was very attractive. Babylon came to mean the British police, the system of unemployment benefits, the government, big business, in fact any part of the "system" which was seen to be oppressive.

All of these sentiments were not only expressed in the lyrics of the music, but were also found in the way that the music was played. Just as white musicians in the 50s took blues and gospel and made it their own, Reggae artists evolved their music from the elements of Rock. Most rock music is based around a basic four-beat bar. The emphasis is upon what is called the off beat, or back beat. So the snare drum will hit beats two and four. In reggae this rhythmic pattern is turned upside down. The back beat disappears and the snare drum is hit on the third beat of the bar. In this way black musicians effectively created a musical or cultural rebellion against white domination by taking white music and twisting it to their own ends.

Interestingly enough, Reggae itself was subsequently taken up by white young people. In the late seventies it was very often to be found being played in the venues where Punk acts performed. At the end of the Punk era The Police used reggae rhythms in most of their early hits. In their hit "So Lonely" they use a reggae beat in the verse but break into a straight rock beat for the chorus. The Police were massively successful but, with a predominately white middle-class audience, needless to say their lyrics never expressed the same sense of alienation and rebellion that is found in real Reggae. In the 80's middle-class young people, who have always been attracted by issues of conscience, were most likely to be the ones listening to Bob Marley, even if they couldn't understand the words!

N.W.A.

Rap music started when groups of black young men on the streets of New York and other cities in the US began to compete with each other by chanting lyrics at each other. These raps were always a celebration of how important, clever, wise, sexually desirable, or physically strong they were. Of course this was an assertion of power in a situation that most people would see as being right at the bottom of American society. But that was the point – in a tough situation pride is an understandable defence. These claims were made over and against the mainstream of white culture which surrounded them.

As these musical styles developed, interaction with traditional middle-class values was carried into the way the music itself was developed. It has always been a matter of some importance to white middle-class young people that their musical heroes can really "play". Thus Eric Clapton was proclaimed as "God" simply because of his ability to play lead guitar. In contrast to this kind of attitude these black rap musicians began to develop ways of making music without any of these traditional musical skills much prized by white young people.

One way of doing this was to lay down a basic beat, to rap over, by making percussive sounds with your mouth. This was called beat box and with the aid of a microphone it could be made to sound very effective. Perhaps a more conscious interaction with white music came with what is called scratching. This is an effect which can be achieved on a record turntable by moving a record back and forwards making different sounds which can be used to create a more interesting backing track to the rap records. A skilled D.J. (disc jockey) can use records in this way to make all sorts of different effects. Here again the idea that you need to be a musician to make good music is turned on its head.

With the advent of digital recording equipment this kind of subversive cultural activity has been taken to new heights. Using a sampler it is possible to lift drum sounds, guitar tracks, even individual words or whole vocal phrases off already recorded music. With all the sophistication of modern synthesizers and drum machines it is possible to construct whole songs from other pieces of music. Black musicians in particular have pioneered these techniques often using classical rock tracks as the basic elements for their own music. Interestingly enough, Led Zeppelin songs have been favourites, particularly for their bass drum sound. But this kind of subversion has not been limited only to the way that music is constructed; there has also been a similar development in use of language by rap acts.

In recent times several rap groups have begun to take normally offensive words and used them as a matter of pride. N.W.A. (N.W.A. stands for "Niggers With Attitude") is one of these groups which has had a good deal of success in this country. The group use the word "nigger" to describe themselves constantly. This has the effect of changing the meaning of the word from one of abuse by white people against blacks into a slogan which is repeated with pride. Some female rap acts have done the same with the word "bitch", using it for any woman who has learned to be assertive and aggressive about her place in the world and about her sexuality. Here, again, a word used by men against women as a term of abuse has been transformed. This ability to change the meaning of words has the effect of throwing the abuse back in the face of the dominant group.

Let's dance

Whether it be Saturday night down at the town hall, or at the local disco or an acid house party on a disused airfield, dancing has always been at the heart of youth culture. Dancing has usually been associated with working-class groups in Britain, although more mainstream middle-class groups can also find discos and balls very attractive. Middle-class rebellious young people will dance, but this is usually at gigs rather than at discos.

Music to dance to is nearly always about sex or relationships. More serious or rebellious issues are not dealt with ordinarily by mainstream dance acts, although there is much crossover between rap music and the club scene. Young people in Oxford start going to the various clubs and discos at about the same time as they break away from their neighbourhood gangs. Young people usually need to look like they're aged 18 and perhaps have some kind of identification to prove they are that age, because the clubs are always licenced. However some of the clubs in Oxford have started to hold mid-week sessions which do not sell alcohol and which are therefore open to those under 18.

Amongst Asian young people there is a very strong emphasis on dances and discos. It has been the habit in Oxford for halls to be hired privately for Asian young people to dance to Bhungra groups. This whole scene is big business; however the dances nearly always take place in the middle of the afternoon and alcohol is rarely, if ever, on sale. All of this provides a safe environment free from racial attack and therefore parents are more likely to allow their young people to attend.

Incidentally, the video scene is very big amongst these Asian young people, possible because their own music and films are hard to come by on regular telly.

One interesting feature amongst these young people is that there is less identification with particular bands. Whereas the name of a group is all important to those who listen to Heavy Metal it is less important or even irrelevant to working-class young people at a disco. Names of bands or acts are never announced at a disco and all the music merges into one. On several occasions I've tried to find out what bands working-class young people are listening to and they haven't been able to name any. Once I asked a young person who was part of a group I was talking to what he was listening to on his personal stereo and he had no idea – in fact, he was a bit puzzled why I wanted to know! For many young people it seems that music is not the all-important thing, it simply provides the environment in which the real action can take place.

In recent years the dance scene has taken yet another interesting turn with the advent of the "Manchester Scene". Bands such as The Happy Mondays, James, The Stone Roses, and Inspiral Carpets have taken the basic dance format and fused it with a more rock sound. This mix has found some popularity amongst middle-class young people as well as some working-class groups. The lyrics of their songs quite often express a dissatisfaction with life and are tinged with a more psychedelic drug feel reminiscent of the sixties. In fact, fashion has followed this trend in a fusion of the more tracksuit-based style of dress, worn by black young people, with psychedelic tee-shirts tie-dyed in the old hippy manner.

Why should the devil have all the good music?

Every attempt by Christian artists to make rock music to date has fallen at one of several hurdles. Firstly, good popular music has always arisen in relation to a genuine youth subculture. Whichever musical movement you think of, be it punk, reggae or rap, there has always been the sense that it expresses the real tensions and concerns of a particular group of young people. It's this relationship which has given the music a cutting edge, both in terms of its message, and in terms of its eventual meaning to young people.

Membership of the Christian Church and community has usually meant that Christian musicians have been dislocated in some way from the very context in which genuine creativity can take place. As a result Christian music has often only appeared to be a copy of the real secular scene. Such copies have often been inferior and are usually about five years out of date.

This separation between the Christian community and the wider youth culture has also meant that much of the alienation and angst that youth cultures are fuelled by is not experienced first-hand by Christians. If Jesus answers all your problems, then the sense of injustice, hurt, aggression, and sexuality that gives rock music its energy is hard to manufacture. Of course, the social problems most young people experience are still there for Christians. But Christian young people often find them hard to identify with, and their faith has given them too few tools with which to interact with them creatively.

One solution has been the creation of a separate Christian subculture. In what is seen as a more safe environment, sanitized versions of Heavy Metal, Rap, and Rock, are offered to what are often exclusively Christian audiences. Rock concerts happen in church halls far away from the regular rock venues in the pubs and clubs. Christian record labels have been set up to fuel this alternative culture. Festivals such as

Greenbelt, which sees itself as having a wider mission, unfortunately, in the minds of the average young person, only serve to fuel the isolation of this rock scene.

I have to come a bit clean here; wearing my hat as a Christian musician I have performed at Greenbelt and Spring Harvest. I have also recorded on a Christian label[1] and performed in many church halls and gigs organized by university Christian Unions in my time – all of which I have enjoyed doing, and I hope to continue to do! But my experience has made me somewhat uneasy about the whole scene. The way forward, it seems to me, is that Christian musicians need to get out of the Christian ghetto, not just to perform in secular venues, which I admit they are doing with increasing frequency. What I'm talking about is a real need to be connected with youth culture at its roots, to be part of what is happening in a particular area, with particular groups of young people. It's only by forging these kinds of relationships, at the grass roots, that Christian musicians can ever hope to be expressing, both in the content of their lyrics and in the form of their musical style, the tensions and concerns of young people[2]. Genuine Christian music will be a music which grows out of these kinds of contacts and seeks to demonstrate how Jesus identifies with them.

NOTES

1. Plankton Records sees its role as being an alternative to the musically safer more mainstream Christian labels.
2. Good examples of this are The Rez Band and Fresh Claim.

8

Magazines

Every youth subculture is really just a different way of consuming. The fact that in the 50s young people were suddenly able to buy things for themselves meant that for the first time a distinctive "youth" style and culture could develop. Ever since that time young people have exercised their right to be consumers. With money in their pockets they have been able to choose how they dress, what music they listen to, and where they go to on a Saturday night. This fact has given birth to multi-million-pound industries all aiming to supply the objects most desired by young people. The list of businesses supported by the teenage consumer is endless but it includes the music industry, the fashion industry, the drinks industry and the cosmetics industry.

Understandably enough these industries will be seeking to influence as many young people to buy their products as they possibly can. Teenage magazines are one of the main ways these industries attempt to influence the teenage consumer, but there are many other ways. On the telly it is interesting to note how programmes and product marketing have become ever more closely linked. "Top of the Pops", that great British institution, is, despite its presence on the BBC, simply a way to plug records to the young. The Top Forty, around which the whole show is based, is just a way of showing the sales of various singles. Thus being Number One means your recording has sold more than any of the others that week. There is, however, an even more direct relationship between "Top of the Pops" and the cash register. It is well known in the music business that a good appearance on the show is a sure way to higher sales, and in fact is the best kind of exposure for an act that there is. But this is even more true for a video shown on

"Top of the Pops", or for that matter any TV show aimed at the young. The video is referred to by record companies as a "pop promo" and more money is usually spent on it than was spent on recording the song it illustrates! But this kind of product marketing on the TV is not just confined to music. The whole Teenage Mutant Ninja (Hero) Turtles phenomenon, which was much in evidence during 1990, took off as a craze when it was shown as a cartoon series on a children's programme. From this, younger teenagers and children have been persuaded to buy every kind of product imaginable which can have a turtle printed on it. The other day I went to a party and drank from a Turtle paper cup!

Too much pressure

Many of us, seeing all of this advertising aimed at young people, get very uneasy. There seems to be so much pressure on young people to buy things nowadays. But before we get too self-righteous about all of this, perhaps we should take a look at our own life styles; are they really so different?

Two factors have been crucial to the development of the teenage consumer. The first is the availability of spare money produced in the post-war prosperity. The second is the leisure time offered to young people, which has enabled them to take such spectacular advantage of what has been offered to them. These two things – spare money and free time – would be seen by most of us as largely positive developments, not only for teenagers, but for everyone. We want to see a rise in general prosperity and the quality of life and we also want to see more free time in which to enjoy our good fortune. So before we bemoan the fact that young people are the "victims" of tremendous pressures, we have to admit that they are only doing what we as adults have been directing most of our energies towards as well!

If I went through the average night watching telly I would have to admit that my own tastes in entertainment are often just as prone to commercial pressures. "Wogan", for instance, is simply a way of plugging books, films, and TV shows, and

Barry Norman is very witty and nice, but he is really selling us movie tickets. The same is true of BBC-2's "The Late Show", however highbrow it may be, it is still just plugging art, and however picturesque and enjoyable "Holiday '91" may be, it is still an advert for the travel industry. The same is true of the papers and magazines which I devour on a Sunday, they are full of adverts (mind you, I'm not about to buy a BMW just yet!).

It is hard to talk about the pressures young people are under today without admitting that we too are under similar pressures. But I have to also admit that I quite like watching these films and reading these magazines. I like to know what is happening in the world of fashion or holidays, or what wine I should drink with the latest recipe. So I have to confess that if young people are victims of advertising pressure then these pressures simply reflect values I also embrace to a large extent. But if this is the case then I am helping to contribute to the "pressures" that teenagers are under by subscribing to a society that embraces these kind of values.

Spoilt for choice

It's often argued that young people are unfairly exploited by "commercial" interests. Teenage fashion is a very good example of this. We only have to wander around one of our city-centre shopping arcades to see how much is on offer to these "style"-conscious consumers. Each month sees new trends and more expensive temptations for young people to acquire. Egged on by TV advertising and teenage magazines young people are urged to buy one "image" and "look" after another. But these "pressures" are also only really understood if we accept the fact that they represent the interests and values of our adult society. Fashion is an adult construction which supports an adult economy. Most of us are more than pleased with the fact that we are able to buy so many different things in our shops. In fact, we see variety and choice as an important end of our economic prosperity. That young people are under "pressure" to consume is only the other side of the coin to our own rejoicing in a more materialistic way of life.

So once again, even as we bemoan the fact that teenagers are under pressure to consume, we have to take some responsibility for the fact that we have, by our own acceptance of these improvements in our way of life, partially caused these pressures to exist. The pressures young people are experiencing are simply the result of a way of life that we as people living in Britain have consistently chosen to pursue.

Message in a bottle

Teenage magazines are not just a way of putting pressure on young people to buy things. A close inspection will show that along with the cosmetic articles and the self-improving diets and the hero worship of the latest pop idol comes a set of assumptions about life. These magazines in particular have fairly well-defined views on the various roles that young men and women should take in the world. What follows is a brief description of the kinds of images of women and men that can be found in these magazines:

1. Girlies and the stars

The first few pages of a magazine like *Just Seventeen* or *Smash Hits* are always crammed with pictures of men. Of course they are not just any old set of blokes, because these are "Stars". Groomed and studio-styled, they adopt the role of the teenage idol with casual ease. Their lives are full of excitement and action, they star in films, go to parties, holiday in the Bahamas and perform in front of millions of screaming fans. The message is obvious: these men are to be adored, swooned over, dreamed about, idolized. Rarely do we get told about the real person for their lives are usually deliberately trivialized. Interviews and articles treat us to a random array of non-information. We are told how big their feet are, what they wear in bed, when they last kissed someone, what their favourite colour of underwear is. Despite the pretence of intimacy, these magazines tell us nothing about these people which will give us a clue as to what they are really like. But in a way that is the point. These men are being marketed as idols, not people. Any hint of real humanity, weakness or personality would spoil the image. Idols are to be worshipped, but always from afar.

In contrast, the role of the female is to be the worshipper, the one who bursts into tears, screams and yells when she comes face to face with her idol. The young women in these magazines are usually referred to as girlies, chicks or gurls. By any stretch of the imagination these could not be described as very flattering terms. But they ensure the reader knows her place. She is expected to be a fan, to enthuse about the latest man to come along and, of course, buy the record and the tee-shirt and the posters, not forgetting the inevitable Christmas calendar.

2. *Pretty in pink*

As the young woman flicks through these pages certain messages become very clear. The role of the "girlie" is to make herself as attractive as she can. Before and after shots show her how she too can make herself into something much better and more alluring. Make-up tips, dress tips, and hairstyles are recommended. Wisdom from on high which seeks to guide, discipline and influence, but at the bottom of each page there is the price to pay – "Look good in this skirt £17.99"; "These jeans are all the rage £32.50."

Occasionally there is an article which breaks out of the mould. Careers are discussed or there is an advertisement for some good cause or another. But on the whole young women are urged to busy themselves with their appearance. The message throughout is very straightforward. Women get on in the world by paying attention to their looks. Being pretty and dressed in the latest fashions will ensure success. Of course all this effort is aimed at the boys. Look sexy so you attract the right kind of guy who will make you completely happy.

3. *Everthing a girl could want*

Smiling beautiful faces greet us on every page but it has to be said that these magazines only really represent the style of one type of teenager in British society. Confident and happy with a fairly predictable combination of what most High Street fashion shops have to offer, these young people are the mainstream conformist groups. When we see the occasional picture of black or Asian young people they too are dressed in the same type of standard and safe clothes. There is no real hint of rebellion in these magazines. Here style is not used as a creative way to make a statement about life. Instead it is simply a way to be acceptable and the reader is left with no doubts what are the acceptable limits of experimentation and non-conformity.

It is truly astounding how these magazines choose to ignore the majority of youth subcultures in Britain. When many young people are finding incredibly creative and interesting ways to dress, these magazines seem to be content with the safety of the most ordinary and mainstream groups. It's as if young women are being directed towards a culture which doesn't rock the boat too much and any group that might be even a bit challenging is ignored.

4. *Let's get serious*
Very few "serious" topics are ever dealt with in these magazines. The continuous round of articles about health, fashion, self-improvement, pop musicians, and relationships effectively steers young women into a very traditional role in life. Such subjects as feminism, politics, management skills, creativity and science are rarely, if ever, dealt with. This obviously results in a fairly blinkered perspective, where certain areas of life are seen as irrelevant, or even subliminally "out of bounds".

When "world issues" like famine, disaster and war are dealt with it can often be in a jokey context. Chernobyl, put alongside Bros and Chino trousers as the main events to happen in 1986 is one example which comes to mind. The effect of this is to trivialize and treat as being largely unimportant issues which deserve a little more thought. But then, these sorts of things are best left for the men to deal with, aren't they?

Part of the problem here is the style in which these magazines are written. If you are tied to a format which demands short pithy sentences, lots of slang words, and a jumble of different things in the space of a few column inches, then it is not surprising that there is a lack of reverence for more weighty issues. But the net effect of this is that it simply reinforces the view of women which treats them as being incapable of serious thought and says they are only there as some kind of decoration or amusement.

Interested parties

Reading through the glossy pages of the teenage magazines it's hard to find an article or a story which is not trying to sell something. The advertisers who place these adverts, and therefore provide most of the revenue for magazines, to a large extent dictate their editorial policy.

This kind of influence is never direct, but it is well known that advertisers want their products to be promoted in an atmosphere which they think is conducive to their sale. Thus sensitive political issues are avoided, as are minority issues and alternative viewpoints. The net effect of all this is that the magazines are very concerned to flow with mainstream popular culture, and by doing so they help perpetuate and promote it.

The views of women that are the general pattern amongst the magazines simply represent where our culture is at on this issue. Alternative perspectives on the role of women of course exist, but they are seen by the majority of the population as being a bit odd or even a bit dangerous. It is little wonder therefore that advertisers do not want to sell their products in a way which connect them with these kinds of ideas. This is an important point to take on board, because whilst we may feel ill at ease with the sexism displayed by some of these magazines, we need to recognize that, as opinion formers, we in the Christian Church don't have much to be proud of here – after all women are still refused leadership positions purely on the basis of their sex in most of our Churches.

Mainstream culture and teenage rebellion

As I have said earlier in this chapter it's hard to complain that young people have so much pressure on them to buy, or that they are being unfairly influenced, when everything presented to these readers is really only the standard values of our society. From a Christian perspective there is obviously a good deal to say about these magazines. We could point out the basic materialism that lies behind their viewpoint, but this would sound a bit hollow when we are sitting in our nice, comfortable houses with our video recorders and expensive hi-fis, and with a car parked outside. The problem is that we, like these young people, are part of a society which has certain norms and values. These values affect us and form our behaviour in so many different ways. As Christians we might feel we are "different", but we're still affected by the power of the media and are, in turn, part of the mix which has created these values.

In looking at the various youth cultures that exist it has been evident that not every young person adopts the mainstream values put across in these magazines. Many youth subcultures can be seen as a rebellion against precisely these kinds of values. As Christians we need to recognize that many of the issues which concern these rebellious young people should also concern us. Our problem has been that we have failed to see how Jesus interacts with their concerns, mainly because we have identified Jesus so strongly with mainstream values. This identification can be seen quite clearly if you look at any Christian magazine alongside its secular counterpart. The Christian magazine is really doing the same kind of thing, apart from the fact that it sells Christian books, records and films. Developing relationships with young people who are outside the flow of mainstream culture and seeking to see Jesus through their eyes will give us the new perspectives we so desperately need.

Exercise

This exercise is designed to help you to analyse teenage magazines for yourselves (don't just take my word for it!). The questions are a follow-up to this chapter.

For this exercise you need to go out and buy two or three magazines that are obviously marketed for young people. There are one or two magazines which are primarily bought by boys, such as those dealing with Heavy Metal or some other special interest. These are helpful as a comparison with more mainstream publications, but for this exercise you will need to have in front of you magazines which are mainly bought by girls. For comparison it might also be good to have a Christian magazine to refer to as well.

Spend as much time flicking through these magazines as you can spare. Read any of the articles that catch your eye and try to get a feel for their content and style. When you have done this, try to answer the following questions – it might help you to write down a few notes, or to discuss the questions with a friend.

1. How much material in these magazines is directly or indirectly trying to sell something? Is the Christian magazine any different in this respect?

2. Much of the material in these magazines, directly or indirectly, offers advice to young people. Can you try and summarize the main general themes of this advice? In what ways does the Christian magazine represent an alternative view?

3. Spend some time looking at pictures and articles dealing directly with men. What kind of relationship to these men are the magazines encouraging amongst young women?

4. When these magazines deal with women what kind of roles in life are they promoting for them? How often are women seen only as spectators or sex objects? How often do they encourage women to be creative or active in their lives?

5. Do these magazines ever deal with more "serious" issues or news stories? When they deal with this kind of subject matter what kind of tone is adopted? What message does their approach to these issues convey to young women?

6. If these magazines are bought and read by young women we can assume they have some kind of effect upon the way these young readers view life. In whose interest do you think it is that young women adopt the kind of values you see being presented in these magazines?

9

Sex

Adolescence is defined by sex. The onset of puberty marks the end of childhood in a very physical way. Suddenly your body is developing and maturing sexually, and it is this fact which sets an inescapable agenda for every teenager. The question each of of us has to face is, "How do I make sense of sex?" No one successfully makes it into adult life without answering this question.

In a way you could say that the physical changes brought on by puberty are a kind of challenge. This challenge, however, is made even more difficult by the mere fact that young people begin to develop sexually at a relatively young age. So young men and women are capable of full sexual activity a long time before they have formed any sure sense of who they are. Of course this is obviously going to be the case, because our sexuality is very much at the heart of our personality. So making sense of sex is not just a physical problem, it is more importantly a question of what it means to be an adult. It is a question of identity not physiology.

A thoroughly Christian concern

Christians have always been concerned about issues related to sex. In the area of youthwork much effort has been spent by Christians to present and explain the "Christian" viewpoint on this particular area, i.e. don't do it unless you're married. The problem with much of the Christian material on this subject is that it doesn't really interact fully with the question of identity. We need to realize that every young person has to establish their own sexuality within a network of relationships. Just as there are different patterns of friendship amongst different groups of young people, there are also a considerable variety of social contexts in which young people seek to work out their sexual identity.

If we are ever going to be able to present a "Christian" perspective on sex to young people then we cannot simply limit our comment to the physical act of intercourse. Neither should we fall into the trap of assuming that sex has the same meaning for every group of young people. In fact the meaning of sex and sexual activity is fundamentally affected by issues related to class and gender. If you are a working-class girl growing up on a large council estate the chances are that you will experience sex in a totally different way than a middle-class boy who is heading for university. To understand these differences it is necessary to try to describe the different kinds of relationships which form the context for sexual activity amongst young people.

Love child

Sex for working-class girls can often start very early on in life. It is not uncommon for girls to become sexually active at the age of 14 or even younger. What is particularly disturbing is that very often these girls first experience sex with much older boys. In fact there is a certain amount of prestige attached to being the first to "have" a girl amongst certain older teenage boys – especially if she is under the legal age of consent. It is rare for any such relationship between an older boy and a younger girl to last for more than a week or so, and in some cases it may have just been a one-night stand.

Sex for these girls is often not a pleasurable experience. Some girls admit they have to be drunk before they can bear it and yet they see no other way of attracting boys. Boys are a status symbol which they know they must have if they are to be fully accepted by their friends. But this attitude simply allows the boys to use these girls in any way they wish. In fact more abusive relationships between younger girls and older boys are not uncommon.

I heard of one situation where a group of boys regularly used a van as a place to take girls to have sex. They would park this van outside places where teenage girls hung out and then, in return for drugs, perform a variety of sexual acts with the girls. The drugs, however, did not necessarily represent payment in the girls' eyes, they were just a part of the whole danger of the situation.

For some working-class girls these kinds of exploitative relationships with boys are an inevitable part of their sexual identity. Coming from disrupted and broken homes, these girls see that their mother is being treated similarly by her boyfriends. It is quite understandable then that girls coming from these backgrounds often simply repeat these sorts of destructive patterns in their own relationships.

Slags and studs

For young working-class boys who hang out in gangs, sex nearly always takes place in relationships which are short-lived. One lad talking to me about his mates said they were always on the look-out for girls who were interested. Even when they were "going out" with a girl they would be looking for someone who was more attractive, or more available, and they would have no qualms about sleeping with this other partner. In a way the easy and uncommitted nature of these sexual encounters is explained by the social nature of the gang. When there is such a tight bond amongst the group of friends a relationship of any depth with a girl raises many problems.

One young person told me that for him and his mates sex was the ultimate thrill, but essentially it was like anything else they got up to. You did it for a while and then moved on to the next thing. Of course it was all for the better if the next thing was actually another girl. I was told the story of one working-class lad who was said to have had sex with three different girls at a party. When he went to school the next week this fact was well known by everybody and he was regarded as being someone very special. He was a stud. In fact, even some of the girls at the school were attracted to him because they thought he must have something special!

This attitude to the sexual exploits of boys is very widespread amongst all classes of young people; however the same standards are never applied to girls. If a girl is seen as being too available then she is universally seen as a "slag". This attitude is sometimes used by girls themselves against each other and the fear of being thought a slag is very powerful. I heard of a group of girls who would not carry or use a condom because they thought it meant they would be thought of as being too easy. This sort of behaviour amongst girls who are obviously very much at risk of getting pregnant shows how powerful this kind of attitude can be, but it also shows that sexual activity and patterns are the result of wider social patterns.

In their behaviour working-class girls and boys are simply acting out what they think it means to be adults. In doing so they are not inventing new ways of relating to each other as male and female. The patterns of oppression, power, and abuse I have described are simply an example of how the values and morals of our adult society are duplicated by the young. Unless we are familiar with these values and patterns, any advice offered to the girls or to the boys will be at best naïve and at worst very destructive. We need to recognize that our own values and attitudes to sex may well have been worked out in very different social relationships and patterns to those experienced by these young people.

Love, love me do

Most teenage girls, when asked, will want sex to take place only when they feel that they are cared for. "It's all right if we love each other" is the norm by which the morals of sexual activity are judged. I heard of one group of girls who regularly measure how much their blokes love them, on the basis of where they do it. Thus the car park behind the local supermarket comes only a bit lower than on the grass in the local park – obviously both of these are more satisfactory places for sexual adventures in the summer than they are during the winter! Best of all is the chance to do it in a bed or even in the back of a car. For a very pretty girl who is high up the "pecking order" to do it in the park might be considered to be a bit of a disgrace. This kind of ladder of worth has hidden behind it certain "class" implications.

It's fairly obvious that for young people who are sexually active finding a place to have sex is quite a problem. I knew of one couple who regularly on their way home from the pub used to make love on the steps of the Oxford University Library in Radcliffe Square, a place not usually associated with carnal knowledge! In measuring their worth by the venues which various blokes can provide where they can make love, the girls are in effect talking about the relative status of their boyfriends. After all, it makes sense that a more wealthy, and older, middle-class boy is going to have regular access to a car. The same is true of the ultimate venue – a bedroom. Middle-class boys are more likely to be able to provide an empty or large house which can give the necessary privacy for sex to take place in comfort.

Going out

Amongst middle-class young people the one-night stand is still a feature of their relationships. Most often this sort of thing will take place at a party or after a visit to the pub but it is usually a feature of those in the middle years of adolescence. It is not uncommon amongst these groups of young people for the sexual partners, indulging in a one-night stand, to each be part of the same group. They may well see each other as part of the larger group both before and after the "evening". This does not seem to cause too much tension for middle-class young people, who will often quite happily relate to each other much as they had before they got off with each other. However with working-class lads it is unheard of for them to give any time or attention to a girl whom they have had sex with on a one-off basis – in fact their presence is likely to be hardly acknowledged at all if they show up again.

Going out is a feature of early – and late – adolescence for most middle-class young people. Around the ages of 13 or 14 it is considered to be essential that you have a boyfriend or a girlfriend. These early relationships may not last more than a month or two, but they are where the first sexual experiments take place. Obviously many things are there to be tried, without "going all the way" and young middle-class teenagers may be fairly content, for quite some time, with the delights of various kinds of foreplay.

More committed relationships are returned to, if they have ever been abandoned, in the later teenage years (17–19). Middle-class young people are very likely to form very close and intense attachments as they get older. These relationships can last for several years and involve a large measure of intimacy. Sex need not always play such an important part of these friendships. It seems that after young people have experienced sex with a few people they are, by this time, much more interested in loving mutual friendships which are much more supportive.

Virgin records

Every teenager is curious about sex, so it is not surprising that losing your virginity is an important milestone. Many young people I know find it very hard to understand some of the Christian young people who have decided not to have sex before they are married. A virgin, to be honest, is a rarity amongst most 16, 17-year-old young people. In fact, to them, what's important about virginity is losing it.

I heard of one group of working-class lads who had amongst their group one boy who had never had sex. This became quite a challenge for the group! The boy was told in no uncertain terms that unless he had done it by the time he was 18 the gang would club together and take him to a prostitute. I knew of an older middle-class couple where the girl was much more experienced than the rather shy boy. It was fairly well-known by the group that this situation existed – in fact much fun was had talking about the various plans and ruses that the girl dreamed up to get the boy into bed. The remarkable thing was how long this situation went on without the girl having any success. Evidently not every boy is just out for what he can get. I heard of another middle-class couple who conspired to give their friends the impression that they were having sex. Neither of them felt ready for sex, so they agreed to mislead their friends rather than stand out from the crowd!

These stories should only serve to show that young people are individuals and that any generalization about them should be taken with a pinch of salt. That said, however, it is true that there is considerable pressure for young people to be sexually active from a relatively early age.

Sex and power

The general assumption that men are somehow superior to women may not be accepted as a general philosophy nowadays, although in sexual matters the true relationships between the sexes can be clearly seen. In a number of ways the general social patterns of relationships amongst young people display the fact that boys have things more in their favour than do girls, though this is not always the case.

It has been a normal pattern in history that women have used sex as a means of gaining power in their relationships with men. The male suspicion of women's sexual power, very much encouraged by the Christian Church in its reading of the Adam and Eve story, has been the source of much injustice and prejudice. However, some girls today still see sex as one way that they can gain the upper hand.

Sex for working-class girls is one of the main ways they can get any hold over the boys they go out with. The same pattern can be seen amongst middle-class girls who are often willing to give sexual favours simply to keep a boy whom they feel strongly about. I heard of one group of girls who had the attitude that sex was a way to keep a guy hooked. This was seen as being most useful as a strategy if the boy offered certain social advantages. Perhaps he had a car or he had money enough to take them out regularly and buy them things when they wanted them. Needless to say, what might seem as a clever strategy for self-gain on the part of the girls simply repeats the general pattern of our society where a woman is seen as needing a man to provide for her. This is to some extent enshrined in the marriage service where a father "gives" the girl away to the husband. This ritual is still gone through, and seen as being perfectly normal, even if the girl has left home for several years.

A game of consequences

It is fairly obvious that for young women the odds are much higher when it comes to sex. When the guy may be long gone the girl may have to face the problem of an unwanted pregnancy. It should be obvious from what has so far been said that teenage pregnancies are increasing at an alarming rate.

Neglect of any contraceptive protection is very common amongst young people. Most experience sex for the first time without any protection. This is even the case when the boy is much more experienced and should know better. In some cases this is because of ignorance; more often than not, however, it is because many young people find it hard to imagine it will ever happen to them. This is, of course, very unrealistic, but being responsible about sex is a major part of the challenge of becoming adult.

The fear of AIDS has given a much higher profile to the humble condom and at least one result of this terrible disease is that every young person knows what one is! But it must be said that many young people regard AIDS as being a very distant threat, if they even think about it at all.

Most groups of young people are fiercely heterosexual. I work in an all-boys school and it is very common for boys to be called "bent" or "queer" if they step out of line in any minor way from the established norms. Homosexuality is regarded as totally outside all comprehension. This is probably because there is a great deal of insecurity and fear which surrounds all of our attempts at establishing a sexual identity. The same kind of attitudes can be found amongst teenage girls. I heard of one group of girls who were so disgusted by scenes of lesbian sex on a recent BBC drama series that they turned over and in one case even switched off the telly – a very unusual act for any teenager!

Given this general atmosphere it is not surprising that young people who feel their sexual orientation is towards people of their own sex very rarely express this until they are in their later teenage years. It is not at all uncommon for young people who later "come out" to have had boyfriends and girlfriends and even to have experimented with heterosexual sex on more than one occasion before their sexual preference becomes clear to them. Some young people do find ways to come to terms with their obvious "difference" to their friends. I have known some teenage boys who have deliberately dressed in more effete ways and have found that by adopting a general intellectual and artistic "camp" manner they are accepted, especially amongst more rebellious middle-class groups.

Living on the edge

As adults seeking to be friends with young people issues to do with sex are inescapable. There are innumerable situations where the traditional Christian teaching about sex seems to leave us ill-equipped to deal with much that young people experience in their sexual lives. Issues to do with contraception, sex below the age of consent, abortion and homosexuality are very tricky to sort out indeed, even if you are approaching the issues from a Christian standpoint. But when you are trying to help young people who may not be Christian, and who therefore probably don't share the same moral perspective, the situation becomes even more complicated.

Friendship seems to be a good place to start looking at some of these issues. Friends are never uncritical; in fact their advice, when it is asked for, is very much to be prized. But the first rule of friendship is loyalty – especially when times get tough. This kind of friend will stand by you and be a support when things go wrong, even if she/he thinks you have been doing something thought to be unwise. If a girl has become pregnant and has decided to have an abortion then, whatever view about this issue I may hold as a Christian, my place as a friend is to be alongside her helping her to make the best decision she can within her framework before the termination, and afterwards I should be there to show care and sympathy. Needless to say, as a man I would always ensure that the primary role in this kind of caring is taken by a responsible woman.

Being friends with non-Christian young people will involve us in being part of decisions about sex which are taken on a basis very different to our own. It is not our place to impose our values and morals on young people who don't share our beliefs. It is not uncommon, of course, for young people to ask what you would do in a certain situation, but that doesn't mean they will do the same! Indeed, talking about waiting until you get married before you have sex is shutting the door after the horse has long bolted!

If we are really going to be of help to young people we need to be able to share a Christian approach to sex which takes full account of where they actually are at, instead of where we feel they should be at. If sex is more a matter of identity than it is of physiology then it is probably at this point that we need to start. Sex is a precious gift but it needs to be used wisely and responsibly.

For many young people their very low sense of self-worth means that any kind of "responsibility" around sex is extremely difficult. For instance, a 14-year-old girl, who has slept with a 19-year-old boy at a party, may well not be helped by someone telling her she has committed a sin. This is not the place to start; in the first place there is a sense in which she has been sinned against by the older boy. From the older boy's point of view his lack of respect for the girl may well have its roots in his own low self-image. But she and the boy are also trapped in a very destructive social pattern, which they didn't invent but inherit. This does not mean they are not responsible for their actions, or that having sex outside marriage is somehow all right for them. The point is, if we are going to help either the boy or the girl then the place to start will most probably have to be with the question of identity and self-respect.

Role model

In Jesus's dealings with sexual issues, he seems to have been able to help people to value themselves – yet at the same time he didn't underplay the crucial issue that sex belongs within marriage.

The woman taken in adultery (John 8:1-11) is a good case in point. Jesus first focuses his attention on the men who are so quick to condemn this woman. The fact that they are willing to use her disgrace as some cheap theological argument shows they know very little about the value of people. Jesus, however, neatly pops their bubble by challenging each one to look at their own sinfulness. When he looks up at the woman he does not condemn her, and yet he says, "Go, but do not sin again." Somehow you feel that after this encounter with Jesus the woman will be changed and indeed will not end up committing adultery again. Jesus in action and words has assured her of her value before God, even in the midst of sin, and it is this assurance which will fuel her changed life.

For many young people a responsible attitude to sex can only come when they have learned to love and respect themselves. This kind of change of life is at the heart of the Christian Gospel, it grows from an encounter with Jesus. This is where our friendship as adults really comes in. Young people need to see the power of Jesus at work in our lives, to bring wholeness and a sense of self-worth, before they will reach out to Jesus themselves.

But it also needs to be said that young people learn self-worth from us. If we treat them as being valuable then, over time, their image of themselves will change. It is only within these sorts of relationships that we can say anything useful about sex to young people. From a distance we can say what we think is right, but if we want to help young people to grow into Christ in a whole way then we must get involved.

PART III

*

The Big Picture

10

Why Doesn't Jesus Preach the Gospel?

In my experience there is nothing as challenging or as exciting as sharing the Good News of Jesus with young people. Getting to know a group of young people over a period of time lets you into a world which is, at one and the same time, so rich in creativity, and so poverty-stricken in its cries for recognition. Real friendship with teenagers affects you, it opens your eyes to things you have never seen before. Some of these things will be very positive and others you will never wish to see again. But whatever experiences come your way the question which will always be there in the background is "How does the Gospel of Jesus relate to these young people?" Answering this question in a way which really interacts with the background and culture of the teenager is a big challenge! But before we can do this effectively we need to look at what exactly the "Gospel" is.

Relying on a formula

Reading the average guide to evangelism there seems to be an assumption that the Gospel is one simple and basic message which we should try to get over to people. Some call it the ABC, others the "Four Spiritual Laws", but whatever it is called it is always presented as a simple "formula". This formula always assumes that the content of the Gospel is basically a set of ideas. So the task of evangelism is to present these "ideas" in as clear and concise a form as possible. The theory is that the potential convert must first understand these ideas, then accept they are true, and act upon their content. So evangelism simply becomes the explanation of a set of ideas or concepts. These ideas or concepts are called "the Gospel". This, in a nutshell, is "evangelism", according to the guides.

Given this view of "the Gospel" there is little need to take any notice of issues related to culture, since it doesn't really matter who you are dealing with and what their background is, because the "formula" is the "Gospel" and therefore it is true for everybody. You only need to gain enough understanding of people to communicate what is essentially a very simple message to them.

For sometime now I have felt that this approach to the Gospel (let alone to people), has severe problems built into it, especially when you compare it to how Jesus related to people. Quite early on in my Christian life I began to get very puzzled by the kind of things Jesus said and did. As I read the first three gospels I could not get out of my mind the uncomfortable reality that he did not preach according to the Gospel formula I had been taught was universal and unchanging. Of course I realized that Jesus had not died on the cross that early in the story, so how could he preach a message about it? But this fact in itself didn't satisfy. The gospels were written after the death and resurrection of Jesus – in fact they assume these facts all the way through. So I couldn't dismiss the ministry of Jesus as being before the "Gospel" formula was created. Neither could I accept that Jesus himself was ignorant of the Gospel "facts" and that was why he failed to tell people the Gospel in more clearly-formulated terms.

As I thought about this more I began to wonder if I was starting in the wrong place. After all, the gospels and the life of Jesus must carry more authority than an evangelistic pamphlet or formula. Following this line of reasoning I went back to the gospels and tried to look at how Jesus related to people. I made a summary of everybody he met and everything he said or did when he met them. The results were pretty mind-blowing.

Looking at Jesus

As I studied the gospels a pattern began to emerge that I found both challenging and very helpful. Jesus says different things to different people. He didn't have a formula that he attempted to get everyone to accept. In fact, the picture of Jesus that comes over in the gospels is of a person who deals with people on an individual basis. By this I mean that Jesus took account of the social situation, religious background, and relative position in life of everyone he came into contact with. To a rich man seeking acceptance he says one thing, to a widow facing starvation and death, another. Sometimes it is very hard to reconcile the different things Jesus says to different people. But what is very clear is that he varied his messages and actions to take account of the different people he met. In fact Jesus seems to be very much aware of what it meant to be poor, or powerful, religious or a sinner, and he acts and speaks in the light of this knowledge. In short, the "Gospel", as displayed in the ministry of Jesus, is not a static set of ideas, but a relationship.

In the rest of this chapter I will explore how Jesus displayed the "Good News" in a "relational" way by looking at a number of situations where he treats people very differently. But so this doesn't simply become an interesting "historical" exercise in biblical study I have applied each situation to an issue.

Pointing out sin

One of the trickiest problems in any friendship is knowing when to speak and when to keep silent. Being a friend of young people will inevitably involve a certain amount of tension about this issue. For example, you might be at a party where someone you know is smoking dope, or maybe with a group of teenagers who decide to steal something from a shop. It is very hard to know what to do in these situations, because whatever you do will be wrong with someone or other. So it is quite comforting to know that Jesus wrestled with similar issues in his ministry:

a) ZACCHAEUS: The story of Zacchaeus (Luke 19:1–10) is a remarkable tale of repentance and faith. This man was obviously a very great sinner. He had cheated, stolen and extorted money from so many people that he was universally hated. Of course, tax collectors had to force people to pay a certain amount over the going rate, that's how they made their money. But this did not excuse the sin of this man, and we can be certain about his guilt because at the end of the story he promises to pay those he has cheated four times what he owes them.

When we look at how Jesus treated this man a remarkable fact becomes clear – he did not tell Zacchaeus to repent. He didn't tell him how much God loved him and wanted him to come and be forgiven. Instead, Jesus went home with Zacchaeus and had a meal with him. Eating with someone in Jesus's time was a highly symbolic gesture and showed a deep personal link. When Jesus walked into Zacchaeus's house and sat down at the table God's forgiveness was incredibly real. But here comes the tricky bit. Jesus ate with Zacchaeus before any act of repentance or confession had taken place; indeed, he offered his presence, i.e. the presence of the Kingdom of God, as a free gift.

Jesus knew this man was a notorious sinner. He also knew that tax collectors were regarded as worse than animals by the Jews. After all, they were betraying their own kind by collecting taxes for the occupying power, the Romans. But Jesus chose not to condemn this man, or even to preach to him about how much he had sinned. Jesus was content to accept Zacchaeus, and it was out of this love and acceptance that an amazing repentance came.

b) TAKING TEA WITH A PHARISEE: Although Jesus gained a certain reputation for eating with sinners and outcasts (Mark 2:15), he also was willing to eat with those who were more respectable. In the story of Zacchaeus, Jesus, by his mere presence, brings about new life. However, when he visits the Pharisee (Luke 11:37–53) all of the loving acceptance he shows to the tax collector seems to go out of the window!

Suddenly gentle Jesus, meek and mild, is speaking out. He is willing to condemn people to their face – actually, by most standards, he is insulting and extremely rude. Can you imagine yourself trying out some of Jesus's lines in the home of your local bishop, or church leader! It's pretty outrageous to call a religious leader a fool or a stinking grave, but Jesus did. These people were insulted and upset by the things he said; this is not the warm and friendly Jesus we saw with Zacchaeus. Here we see a person willing to stand up for what he believes is right, a man who sees sin and error and is not afraid to point it out.

Evidently Jesus related differently to Zacchaeus than he did to these Pharisees, but what do we make of this? The first point is that Jesus makes it clear that his priority is for those people considered as sinners. As he says, "I have not come to respectable people but outcasts" (Mark 2:17). As a result of this attitude, when Jesus comes into contact with the "religious" people there is nearly always conflict. Jesus does not seem to shy away from this conflict, but is in fact quite prepared to point out their error and to teach that their attitudes are to be rejected by his followers (Matthew 23:1–27). However, this kind of condemnation is confined almost entirely to those who call themselves "religious".

Coming back to the specific problem of when to point out sin and when not to, using Jesus as our model is very instructive. In the situations I described, i.e. young people taking drugs, or shoplifting, trying to do what Jesus did would mean we would not speak out or condemn these young people. We might not even mention that what they had done is wrong and we certainly should not report them to the police. This kind of strong behaviour is only, it would seem, to be used when dealing with church leaders!

Caring for physical and spiritual needs

A great many young people have very deep social or physical needs. Being a friend of a homeless teenager, or one suffering from physical abuse, demands more than just a "spiritual" message about God's love – there is obviously a need for some practical caring. But for most Christians involved with young people the relationship between practical caring and "spiritual" challenge is a real problem. Some have solved this issue by separating caring from evangelism and, depending on their particular theological bent, push either one or the other exclusively.

In marked contrast to these kinds of compromise Jesus seems to hold these two areas together:

a) THE TEN LEPERS: In the story of the ten lepers (Luke 17:11-19) we see Jesus dealing with a terrible physical ailment. But as the story develops it becomes obvious that he is also concerned about "spiritual" issues. When the one man returns to thank Jesus we are left in no doubt that this kind of response is not only the right one, it is in fact expected. The message seems clear – the goal of healing and practical caring should be the explicit worship of Jesus as Lord.

But the other nine men were still healed. Jesus gave his healing touch before there was any evident response of faith or worship on the part of all ten men. In a way this generous free giving of the precious gift of healing shows something of the truth of God. As Paul puts it, "while we were still sinners Christ died for us" (Romans 5:8).

This kind of open giving and generosity which we see time and time again in Jesus's ministry contrasts very strongly with our own tendency to lay conditions on our care for others. As a form of evangelism we often want to make a specific link between our physical caring and a spiritual challenge which demands a response. Jesus, on the other hand, gives his healing touch to all ten before he knew how they would eventually respond to him.

b) THE PARALYSED MAN: In this story (Luke 5:17–26) Jesus begins straight away with the issue of "spiritual" need by talking about forgiveness of sins. In a way you can imagine the disappointment in the man if he was expecting to be healed and instead Jesus forgave his sins! But Jesus does not stop with a purely "spiritual" renewal of this man's life because he does eventually heal him. In the previous story we saw faith and forgiveness coming to only one of the ten lepers even though all were healed. Here there seems to be an essential link between the two. Somehow we get the impression that without the forgiveness of sins this man would not be whole, even if he was physically healed.

It is hard to escape the fact that in Jesus's ministry concern for people's physical condition is a matter of very great concern. But there is equally great emphasis on more "spiritual" issues like the need for forgiveness and a right relationship with God. What is even more interesting is that these stories show how Jesus clearly saw a relationship between physical care and "spiritual" challenge, but he did not seem to prioritize one over the other. In fact, both his healing and his forgiveness are seen as essential parts of the "Good News".

Returning to the specific issue of homeless teenagers or young people who have been physically abused, we need to be wary of any approach which isolates physical and spiritual issues from each other. Like Jesus we need to treat young people as "whole" people and that means caring for them in both a physical and spiritual sense. But there is one further point here – Jesus doesn't put a higher priority on one of these over and against the other. In other words, caring for the physical needs of a homeless person is an essential part of the Gospel to that young person and it is valuable even if there is no response of faith on that young person's part.

Jesus is the message

When we compare the different ways Jesus related to people in the gospels, the variety is baffling. Sometimes he challenges people to repentance, sometimes he condemns people for their callousness, other times he just spends time with people. What, however, is common to all of these situations is that these people met Jesus and he changed them. This in a sense is the "Gospel" – it is the Good News which Jesus brings to each of us when he meets us. The "Gospel" therefore is not a set of ideas about Jesus, but a relationship with him.

As Christian people who are seeking to share the Gospel with young people we have the amazing privilege of being part of the process by which Jesus comes into a relationship with each individual teenager. As such, we need to realize that confining our activity to simply putting over a few facts about Jesus is not enough. Just to understand the basic outline of the message is not enough – conversion is about meeting Jesus and deciding to follow him. This is a much more concrete and particular reality than can ever be presented in a mere formula. Jesus is a living person who wants to meet young people in the present and show his love and concern in their lives. Our role is simply to provide the context of friendship where this can take place.

There are two more things to say at this point by way of a summary:

1. The Gospel story

When we come to share the Christian faith with young people we start with the gospel record about Jesus. It is, of course, possible to summarize this "story" – it's about God the Father who loved us so much that he sent his Son; it's about Jesus who became a human being, died on the cross for our sin and rose again from the grave; it's about the new life we share with the risen Jesus through the power of the Holy Spirit.

What we need to recognize is that this record of the "facts" about Jesus is not all there is to say. If we spend all our time trying to communicate just these basic facts, then we will be presenting a dry and dead message. Jesus is alive, risen, free and that's how he wants to meet young people.

2. Experiencing the Gospel

Jesus met people in different ways. He was able to respond to the particular social, spiritual, and psychological situations of the people he met.

Our own experience with young people in Oxford is that Jesus meets them in different ways. Some have an incredible inward experience of the presence of God, others feel a deep need for forgiveness, while others just want to become part of what they see as going in an exciting direction and some are delivered from evil. Jesus meets young people in different ways and our calling as youthworkers is to try to learn to do the same. We need to help young people to see how Jesus can be a real part of their lives.

The Jesus who lived, died and rose again needs to come and become a risen presence in their lives. Our role is to enable this to happen, we cannot control it or direct it. Jesus says it himself in John 3:8, when he is trying to introduce Nicodemus to the idea of being born again. He says, "The wind blows wherever it wishes; you hear the sound it makes, but you do not know where it comes from or where it is going. It is like that with everyone who is born of the Spirit."

Exercise

It's worth spending some time reading through the gospels trying to sort out how Jesus related to different people and how he ministered to them in their particular situations. There's no substitute for reading all of one gospel, but the references below are given for those who want to get right at it.

One major clue to how Jesus related to people has to do with their position in society. Ask yourself: does this person have power, were they rich or poor, were they respected or not? These sorts of questions will lead you to an understanding of the particular situation of each of the groups listed in this exercise.

1. WOMEN: Mark 5:21–43, Mark 7:24–30, Luke 7:11–15, Luke 10:38–42, John 4:1–42.
2. TAX COLLECTORS: Matthew 9:9–13, Luke 19:1–10.
3. DISCIPLES: Matthew 18:1–5, Matthew 20:20–28, Luke 22:24–30.
4. PHARISEES/TEACHERS OF THE LAW: Matthew 15:1–9, Luke 11:37–54.
5. THE RICH: Luke 18:16–30.
6. THE SICK: Mark 2:1–12, Mark 5:1–20

11

When Jesus Becomes Real

(i) Starting from the Positive

Friendship is one of the most powerful forces in the world. I remember when I was aged about 16 there was a young man in my local church who took an interest in what I was up to. I realize now that my contact with him was very superficial, but at the time it was so important. Once at Christmas-time he bought me a Christian book and wrote a few encouraging words in the front of it. I can still recall how chuffed I felt when I read what he had written, they made me feel ten feet tall! Somehow this young man's care and friendship had really touched my life. But this is only a partial explanation of what was going on, because there is no doubt that God used the small kindnesses shown to me by this young man as a means to touch my life. Jesus had become real to me, through the friendship.

Friendship and God

Any friendship between an adult and a young person is a possible channel for the grace of God. By this I mean that God uses our efforts at forming friendships as a means to meet with young people and he does this in a free and open-handed way. This is why friendship is the most positive of all places to start Christian youthwork. Of course, by this I don't mean that God is in any way obliged to use this method of outreach, or that an approach based on friendship guarantees "results". What I am saying is that God chooses of his own free will to use our efforts at showing love and concern to young people as a place where he "freely" meets them.

Jesus becomes real to young people when he chooses to do so. We need to hang on to this fact, but we can also say that there are certain aspects of friendship which uniquely reflect the love of God. In other words, there is a kind of symmetry between my actions in showing care for young people and the reality of the grace of God. By showing care to young people I am demonstrating in concrete terms what God is like. I am not by my actions or words making God real to young people – that is a matter for the Holy Spirit. My part in it all is to ensure I am modelling my life and friendship with young people as much as possible on the Good News of Jesus.

Being a friend

Talking about God's grace and friendship with young people makes everything sound very grand and complicated. Actually, friendship which reflects the love of God is nearly always very ordinary and down to earth. Here are a few examples:

1) NAMES: Names are very important things. When I first meet a group of young people it's often where I try to start. Of course, asking a direct question may not be possible and so names may have to be picked up by listening to what other young people call each other. But however you learn a name the fact remains that it is a very personal and precious thing. I know when someone I have only met once remembers my name it makes me feel good, for somehow it shows they know who I am and they think I am worth something. It works the other way round as well; if someone forgets my name when I think they should remember it then I feel a certain amount of resentment. Not surprisingly, names are of crucial importance to young people. I remember one lad getting very angry with me because I'd called him "mate". "You're only calling me 'mate' because you don't know my name," he said with some feeling (unfortunately he was right!).

Being able to call someone by name is just one small, but important, way we can show that they mean something to us. By doing this we are not simply adopting a good youthwork policy, we are actually showing the kind of individual concern and care God has for each of us. God treats each one of us as a person whom he is willing to have a relationship with. Using someone's name is one way of bearing witness to that fact. Jesus uses people's names in just this fashion. Imagine the power of the sentence, "Lazarus come out", or "Hurry down Zacchaeus, because I must stay at your house today." Jesus calls each of us by name and so should we.

2) REMEMBERING: Young people are always willing to talk about the kinds of things that they get up to. It could be that they are playing in an important football match, or going to their sister's wedding, or off to the local swimming baths. It is an essential part of being a friend that we store up these little nuggets of information and return to them when we meet that particular young person again.

Remembering what someone has said and asking them about it the next week or the next day is one vital way of beginning to show you are interested in them and their lives. Whenever a young person shares something, which may seem to us to be of little importance, it is vital we take it seriously. Each of these kinds of throwaway comments is actuallly a window into their lives and what they consider to be important.

Once again, remembering what we have been told and bringing it up at a later date is an effective way to build a relationship but it is also a way of reflecting God's love into the lives of young people. We know and experience the minute care and concern that God is willing to exercise on every part of our lives. Remembering what a young person has told you is just one way of sharing this kind of experience with them. In this way remembering is also a mirror of the Good News of Jesus because it shows we are willing to take the activities, interests and culture of young people seriously. We are not simply out to get them to join in our thing, we want to be part of their world. This kind of journey into their world on our part is an echo, however faint, of how Jesus was willing to live amongst us.

3) BEING A FAN: It is amazing how a few words of praise to a young person can really mean something to them. This could be a simple shout that they have done well from the touchline of a football pitch, or a word after a gig saying how well they played. In fact, many young people are starved of any affirmation, some may never have been told that they look really cool or that they are good at something. This kind of positive influence on young people's lives can be extraordinarily significant. I've known young people, who have considered themselves to be failures and worth very little, change over a period of time to become outgoing and confident about themselves, just because a few adults have consistently got behind them.

Often young people find it hard to be positive to each other – it's much easier to make a joke or a cynical remark – but over a period of time this pattern can be reversed. In my own work with young rock bands, a notoriously critical group, we have always gone a bit over the top in clapping and shouting for more at the end of their concerts. I've noticed recently that this attitude has actually become the norm even amongst the young people themselves.

The net effect of these small gestures of affirmation is an important way to show the love of God to young people. It is fundamental to the Gospel that "God loved us so much that he sent his Son". The force of the word "so" in this passage has the effect of reassuring us that God sees each of us as being of infinite value. It may seem a long way from this idea to a remark about how good a particular lad's hair looks or how good a guitar break may be, but it is not really, for at the heart of each is the tremendous value God places on each of us. By being a fan of young people we are simply finding a way to express God's great love in a very concrete way.

4) DOING THINGS FOR YOUNG PEOPLE: A much-neglected part of friendship is the fact that friends are willing to help you out. Most adults have cars and most young people need lifts. Working with rock bands I often have to carry gear and people to gigs. Sometimes this can be a bit irritating, I must admit, but

it is one way I can do something to help. Another way young people need help is in the area of jobs and references. Going down to the job centre, helping with application forms, or even going along to an interview with a young person to offer support, are just a few of the practical ways an adult friend can be useful to young people. In fact the possibilities for this kind of involvement in their lives are endless! There is also a good deal of mileage in offering this kind of help to young people because it involves you in what they want to do. This takes friendship into a much deeper dimension and gives the opportunity to chat and share in their lives in a multitude of different ways.

Being willing to put yourself out for young people again is a very concrete way to show they are important and valuable. Within the context of a Christian witness and friendship this kind of service says a good deal about the kind of God we worship. In the Bible God is continually seen as someone to whom we can turn to for help; "Give us our daily bread" need not be just a "spiritual" reality. By showing love in very practical ways we are giving young people a very tangible experience of God's goodness.

5) CHATTING ABOUT JESUS: Most of us are a bit too impatient to talk about Jesus. Perhaps because we don't see how significant our actions can be in communicating the Christian faith. My own experience is that even though I may have been in very close friendship with a teenager over a number of years and doing all the kinds of things I have talked about already, there comes a point where I need to talk about Jesus in a very straightforward way. More often than not I'm asked about my faith – perhaps they have heard that I go to church or they overhear a conversation I'm having with one of their friends who has become a Christian. To be honest, the normal reaction to the fact that I'm a Christian is some sort of disbelief or amazement. They are puzzled that someone like me, i.e. someone they know and think of as being generally all right, is even remotely interested in the Church.

I quite like the confusion my faith brings in some young

people for it shows they are having to look at things in a new light. There's a simple process of mental deduction you know is taking place in their minds, "If he's into the Church, then maybe he's not all right. But I know he's all right so why is he interested in church? If he's all right and he goes to church then maybe that means that church is all right..."

Sometimes the subject of church or religion or Jesus never comes up. I find this particularly true when you work, as I do, amongst teenage boys. Conversation is nearly always limited only to the particular game or interest they are taking part in, though sometimes it can stretch to more philosophical issues like will Liverpool win the League this year. After a year or two of joining in this sort of communication I sometimes feel a need to try to expand the horizons of a relationship. I know a lot about their world, but they know nothing about mine. So I occasionally invite individual young people or a small group to come with me to something. Because I'm a Christian musician this will nearly always be some kind of Christian event where I'm playing music. I have to confess that I've never invited a young person to one of these events because I hoped they would "hear the Gospel" and then become a Christian – of course they might – but I have wanted primarily to raise the issue of faith for them. I want them to know a bit more about my life and what makes me tick, but I also want to give them an experience we can both talk about. I've often thought that this was the way Jesus went about his ministry.

I once decided to go through all of the gospels and record the exact circumstances in which Jesus "preached". What I discovered was that in the majority of cases he only spoke in answer to a question. Of course we know of Jesus as a very famous teacher, but his method of teaching was in marked contrast to the way that we are taught in church. More often than not, Jesus gives his teaching in response to an enquiry from one of the disciples, or in response to a contentious question raised by a religious leader. Interestingly enough these questions nearly always come about because Jesus lived in a way which made people ask questions.

6) TALKING ABOUT JESUS IN A GROUP: Some groups of teenagers are actually very talkative. In fact some groups I have known like nothing better than to get together and chat about issues and questions of interest. In these circumstances it is fairly easy to see how some of the more traditional ways of running a "Christian" youth group could be used. But in most circumstances it is best not to take this for granted.

Over the last seven years at Oxford Youth Works we have experimented with all sorts of different types of groups, but they have all had the aim of giving the question of faith in Jesus a much higher profile whilst never moving entirely out of the young people's culture themselves. One of the main problems we have discovered in all this is that as soon as you start to influence a group and take it towards a more formal structure then you will inevitably become some kind of "leader". This need not be a bad thing, but it does mean that the utmost caution must be taken to ensure that whatever is organized remains faithful to the background and particular subculture of the group you are starting to influence.

Kenny Wilson,[1] who works with Oxford Youth Works, has been particularly successful in running this kind of group. Kenny's main group meets in the homes of the various group members. Each week they go from one house to another, and at first the programme included games, a bit of discussion and some kind of Christian talk to round the whole thing up. After a few weeks one of the group came up to Kenny and asked him why he kept putting in the Christian bit at the end of the discussion. Kenny said because he thought it was important, whereupon the young person told Kenny that the group did not like it and wanted him to stop preaching at them. However, the young person went on to say that they all felt Kenny had a perfect right to talk about Jesus within the discussion.

In fact a kind of challenge was issued to Kenny – if Jesus is relevant to everything then whatever we talk about in our discussions, you should be able to apply your faith to that issue. Kenny realized he was trapped on this one! So the discussion went ahead, with the young people now choosing the topics and leaving Kenny free to exercise his right to talk about Jesus as and when he thought it fitted. Remarkably enough, suddenly Jesus became much more real and relevant to these young people than he had ever seemed to be before, because Kenny was forced to think out how Jesus and their concerns were linked.

7) PREACHING AND FRIENDSHIP: I have always felt that at some point in a fully Christian youthwork the Good News about Jesus needs to be "proclaimed". However much youthwork is based on friendship and the culture of young people themselves there should always be a place for the formal preaching of the Gospel. This might seem a bit strange coming after a chapter based on how friendship can be in itself a mirror for the Gospel, but this is not as odd as it may first appear. Whenever we preach the Gospel in our youthwork it is always based on the friendships we already have established with young people. We don't preach to strangers, we preach to friends, and this has a number of very interesting and important implications.

When I talk in an "up-front" way I am speaking to young people whom I know and who in turn know me. In other words, they are able to measure what I say up against how I live. I meet up with these young people most days of the week so I can be held accountable for what I say. In these circumstances I cannot get away with "spiritualizing things" so that they look better than they really are, I can't talk about what I think life should be like, I have to tell it like it really is; I can't paint a picture of being Christian which is too rosy and wonderful, because they will see straight away that I'm not telling the truth. All of this makes the experience of "preaching" to friends a very daunting task, but actually I don't ever find this to be the case.

When I used to travel around to various youth groups and churches to speak I found there was a certain unreality about the whole thing, mainly because I needed to make an impression before I got down to talking about Jesus. Speaking in front of young people I know I don't have to put on any show. I don't need to make up any funny stories or clever jokes or witty phrases for there's no need to make an impression before they are willing to listen to me. My own experience has been that there is no need for any kind of gimmick when you talk to the young people you know, because they want to hear what you have to say. The result of two or three or four years of constant friendship is that they are very open to your experience of Jesus. This, to me, is one of the most important functions of a formal "up front" preach or talk.

Most young people will want to know what you believe and why, but in the ordinary run of things a clear presentation of the facts about Jesus is usually impossible. So there is a great need to find a way to share the whole of the "Gospel" with a group of young people in one go. Our approach to this problem is to run a holiday every Easter where each day we have a short explanation of the Christian faith in, as our advertising pamphlet puts it, "an aggro-free environment". Young people are invited on this holiday if we as leaders feel we know them well enough, and if we feel confident that they will be able to cope with hearing about Jesus in a more structured way. It is a matter of policy that no young person comes on the holiday who is not in a significant relationship with an adult who is also coming on the holiday. In this way the whole "preaching" side of things is built on, and grows out of, friendships which already exist.

But we also want the experience of hearing about Jesus to be related to their everyday situation, both on the holiday, and when they go home. The adult friend is able to make this a much more likely event than if young people came as strangers to our holidays. But this kind of application of the message can also take place in the talks themselves.

When I went to talk to people I did not know, I often found I had to make certain guesses about their lives. I would often try to imagine how I could illustrate my points in a way they could relate to. I would try to make a rough stab at the kinds of issues, concerns and experiences which the people in the audience might have been through. But I never really knew if I was talking about anything which made any sense to them let alone if it was anything which they were at that moment directly concerned with. Preaching the Gospel to young people you know removes all these problems. Suddenly you are able to base the message on issues which are genuine and alive amongst the group.

But there is more to this than topicality. An essential part of the "proclamation" of the Gospel should be an explanation of how the Good News of Jesus is relevant today. This needs to be done in the most down-to-earth and practical way possible. The best way to do this is to take actual events and incidents from the young people's own lives and show how Jesus fits with them. A young person might be particularly self-sacrificing and this incident can serve as a way to explain the cross, another may feel very angry about some kind of injustice and the issue of God's judgement can be discussed. I'm not suggesting you try to correct or put right a young person in a talk, but talking about real events which matter is an essential part of explaining the Good News, and friendship is always a help rather than a hindrance to doing this.

8) FRIENDSHIP IS NEVER CONDITIONAL: If a young person is my friend then they remain my friend even if they hear the Gospel and reject it. My relationships to young people are never conditional on their response to Jesus. This holds true even if a young person professes faith and then drops out. This sort of principle sounds very good, but for it to work in practice there is a need to look at the structure of a youthwork.

When I ran Christian groups I realized I rarely met young people outside a meeting. The net result of this was that when a young person dropped out of the group for any reason then I lost contact with them. In other words, because of the structure in which I was working, I was making the acceptance of the Christian faith, or at least attendance at a Christian meeting, a condition of my friendship with young people.

One way to break out of this is to stop focusing on meetings and start to build relationships. If these relationships involve regular contact on the young people's own territory, then coming to a "Christian" meeting ceases to be such an issue. The young person is free to reject Jesus without rejecting your offer of friendship at the same time.

Starting from the positive

In real friendship there are so many positive starting points which can be a reflection of the Gospel of Jesus. It is vital that we are able to recognize these aspects of friendship, and value them as a genuinely important part of our Christian witness. We will never do this if we insist on separating the more down-to-earth aspects of friendship from the "preaching" side of things. To narrow down the perspective to either one of these is to do much damage to young people and to the Gospel alike.

NOTES

1. Kenny Wilson is employed by Scripture Union in schools.

12

When Jesus Becomes Real

(ii) Starting with Problems

The teenage years can be very traumatic. Making the transition from child to adult is not at all easy and many people experience problems along the way. Getting involved with young people will inevitably mean that we will come across some individuals who are facing really tough issues, often with very little support or help. In these circumstances it is vital we have some idea about what to do, but it is also important that we don't become too problem-orientated in our youthwork. In fact, it is very easy to focus on young people's problems and crises to the exclusion of everything else.

Starting with the positive sides to friendship in the previous chapter, "When Jesus Becomes Real (i)" was a deliberate attempt on my part to place the problems and issues dealt with in this chapter into the much wider perspective provided by long-term friendships. Having said this, however, it is very true that young people often meet Jesus in very real and meaningful ways in the midst of their problems. In this chapter I take some very common problems that young people face and talk about how Jesus can become Good News in these situations. But before that, a word about the professional carers.

The role of the friend and the role of the professional

As a friend it is vital we realize our own limitations. There is nothing more damaging than thinking you can be the total answer to a problem. None of us are Superman or Wonder-woman destined to save the world and it is dangerous to pretend we are. In fact, whatever it is we are trying to help a young person with, there will nearly always be a professional agency or body set up to deal with this sort of thing. We need to learn to guide young people to these professional groups, be they social workers, psychiatric help, or the police. We should never try to handle a serious problem on our own and when we don't know what to do we need to ask for help. This does not mean we do not still have just as vital a role to play as friends.

You can pretty safely assume that most professionals who work amongst young people will not have the time to spend with young people that we have as friends. This is very important because most young people need time to work through issues with someone they trust after they have met with the professional carer. For instance, the health authorities will provide quite extensive counselling and advice for young girls who have abortions, but three weeks after the termination it is the friend who has the time to be there and mop up the tears.

Most professional bodies are set up for a particular purpose. This means they will be governed by a certain set of rules and standards of practice. As a friend you are not so tied down, so there is no reason why you cannot help in a problem of debt or with the repair of a broken-down motor bike. In fact, one problem might well be the occasion for dealing with the other!

But there is another way a friend has a role the professional does not. Helping young people through problems and crises is an important part of our Christian witness. Jesus can become very real to them in the middle of quite horrendous problems. Our role as Christian friends is to learn to be a channel for this to happen. I don't agree with the idea that Jesus takes all our problems away, and I would never offer Jesus to young people as some kind of cure-all Aspirin. However, Jesus does very often show his power in the middle of troubles and problems. The Gospel is all about a God who wants to transform our lives and make them whole.

Family break-up

Parents getting divorced is a very painful event for any young person to go through. Unfortunately the rise in the divorce rate in Britain means that increasing numbers of young people see their homes and their families falling apart. This kind of experience can be incredibly traumatic for a teenager and the scars it can leave may always be with them in one form or another. It is not uncommon for a family bust-up to be at the root of all sorts of adolescent problems including drugs, eating disorders, petty crime, promiscuity, or truanting from school. The stress of parental separation on a young person should never be underestimated.

Young people going through this sort of family break-up need someone to talk to about it. This is where an adult friend can be invaluable. In many cases simply telling someone else that your parents are splitting up can be a great help. In many families there is a great deal of shame surrounding separation and divorce. Teenagers, whether they like it or not, will be affected by this. In some families there has been an attempt to ignore what is going on for so long that teenagers find a real sense of release simply by telling someone else what is really happening.

In families going through separation and divorce young people are always caught in the middle. Dad takes you on one side and tells you "The truth about Mum", Mum has a quiet word "to make sure you are on my side in all this". Teenagers are forced to choose who they will live with. I heard of one boy who had to testify in court on behalf of one of his parents. It is not uncommon for teenagers to end up being blamed for everything that goes wrong in a family, and, even if they are not blamed, some young people carry a deep sense of guilt about their parents' divorce.

It is not unusual for teenagers to feel their parents split up because of something they did. All of this is extremely painful and confusing and so it is important that adult friends can provide a safe and uncritical environment where a teenager can sort all of this out. One thing we have done in Oxford on a number of occasions is get a group of young people together to talk about these issues. What I always find remarkable is that young people from different backgrounds and from different family situations are often very willing to sit around and chat about this sort of thing. In fact, some of those a bit further down the line from those in the thick of it are able to say that there really is a light at the end of the tunnel.

Essentially, family break-up is a death – it is the death of the family itself. And like any death there will need to be a proper grief process to go through – disbelief, anger, bargaining, depression and acceptance[1]. Young people need to be helped through this process and told that what they are feeling is OK and healthy. For some, this will be the first time they have experienced this kind of sadness, and its depth or manifestations may alarm them. Our role as adult friends is to be alongside them offering consolation and counsel where it is needed.

The Gospel is all about death and new life; after the crucifixion comes resurrection. I find this fact very helpful in relation to family break-up. Firstly, because it shows that Christ was willing to bear the pain and suffering of the world – in other words he, like the young person caught up in a painful family situation, suffers innocently. This makes Jesus an ideal person to talk to about what you are going through. It is surprising how many young people will turn to prayer when life gets tough, and if a young person is willing to pray then it is always good to encourage them in this direction.

Jesus experienced pain and rejection and this makes him very approachable to young people going through the break-up of their family. It is also good to let young people know if you are praying for them; if I am going to do this I usually ask the young person if it is all right for me to. Sometimes after a time where they have been particularly open about what is going on I will ask if I can pray for them then and there. This can be a good model for their own prayer. The cross and the resurrection also make it clear that new life only comes by facing up to and going through the pain. Our role is to continually help our teenage friends to go through grief and pain so that they can eventually get on with their own lives in a healthy way. Unfortunately some young people find this process a far from simple one to go through.

Issues of control

When your home is falling apart around you and your parents suddenly seem to be people you can't trust, lasting psychological problems can result. Some of these problems can revolve around ways we seek to control our lives. In teenage girls eating disorders such as anorexia and bulimia are often a direct reaction to tensions in the family. Each of these conditions is very complex and in most cases require trained psychiatric help. However there is a lot an adult friend can do to help young people suffering from these kinds of eating disorders.[2]

Anorexia is, in simple terms, a condition where teenage girls starve themselves by excessive dieting or by eating food and later vomiting it up deliberately. Often this condition is surrounded by a good deal of secrecy. I heard of one girl who would vomit into a plastic bag, which she could easily throw away, to avoid using public toilets where she might be discovered. Bulimia is a pattern of dieting and bingeing, and unlike anorexia, it usually doesn't result in any weight loss. Consequently bulimia is a much more easily-hidden condition, although it may well be much more common amongst teenage girls than anorexia.

Each individual case will be slightly different, so it is unwise to generalize about these kinds of conditions too much. But what can be said is that eating disorders usually involve a measure of unreality and escape. For instance, a girl may convince herself that by going on a diet she is resolving all her problems, be they at school or at home, or with a boyfriend. The reasoning would go, when I am on a diet I am in control because I have reduced the chaos in my life to one area over which I do have control and therefore everything is all right. This kind of argument is, of course, self-deceptive, and some sufferers from eating disorders may well be aware of this fact, but this knowledge does not help them to shake off their behaviour patterns, but may well reinforce them with a kind of self-hatred.

Self-deception amongst many anorexics may extend to them buying clothes that are several sizes too big for them. They may well get to the point where they are unable to "see" themselves as they truly are even when they look in the mirror – what appears to be a pitifully-thin body to you and me, to the girl may appear to be grossly overweight.

In other girls dieting can be associated with trying to be the perfect daughter. Sometimes this can be brought on when a father takes a lover and the daughter feels she is now in competition for her father's affections. Excessive dieting can prevent the onset of puberty. Girls suffering from anorexia may not develop breasts and can cease to menstruate. This in itself may be an attempt to remain a child and escape the responsibilities of sexuality. It also might be the case that the girl may feel she is more acceptable to her parents as a child and so she refuses to grow up. Needless to say a girl who is suffering in this way is trapped in a very destructive pattern of behaviour from which it is very hard to escape.

Any teenager suffering from an eating disorder is much in need of friendship. However, I must say that such friendship is nearly always very time-consuming and can be extremely frustrating. The most important thing that must be done, especially with a young girl who is very thin, is to make sure that they see their G.P. This step in itself is very important for the young person because it introduces a certain measure of reality into the situation, but precisely because of this fact there will almost inevitably be a great deal of resistance, on the girl's part, to taking this step. It is very important that you support whatever medical advice is offered by the G.P. and do as much as you can to encourage the girl to attend regularly any clinic or self-help group the doctor recommends. Most clinics will concentrate primarily on getting the sufferer to put on weight, which is vitally important because anorexics can starve themselves to the point of death. The programme of treatment will involve regular times to weigh themselves and certain diets which will be designed to put weight back on.

A friend in these circumstances can be very helpful in giving support and encouragement. This kind of support may involve you in sitting and listening to long and agonizing descriptions of every mouthful of food that has been consumed. Your teenage friend may appear on your door at any hour in a great state of agitation about how many cornflakes she ate for breakfast or how many peas she left on her plate. All of this can try the patience of a saint, but I suppose that's what we're meant to be!

How deeply any medical programme will go into the reasons behind an eating problem will depend upon the particular clinic concerned. Some simply concentrate on the behaviour of their patients, whereas others will offer some form of therapy. As an adult friend I have always felt that whilst I can offer a great deal of support and help my role is different and complementary to that of a professional counsellor. If a girl is obviously suffering from an eating disorder then she will need to be seeing someone who has more experience and training in this matter than I have. It is also important to realize that working through some of these problems with a young person will involve talking about very private and personal issues and these are usually best dealt with in a situation where there are clear boundaries. These boundaries are as important for the young person as they are for the person counselling. For this reason the adult friend should always try to work in tandem with a counsellor.

Having said this there is a good deal a Christian adult friend can offer. The death of Jesus on the cross is at the heart of the Good News. Most often we see the cross as the means by which our sins are forgiven. This is of course very important, but when dealing with a young person suffering from an eating disorder the forgiveness of sins is not the place to start. One reason for this is that their own sense of guilt about their problem is just reinforced by talking about their sin. It is much better to see Jesus as a friend who is willing to walk alongside the young person as they try to work their problem out.

If the young person can begin to relate to Jesus **as a friend** then a number of things begin to follow. In the first place the experience of being loved by Jesus can be a real factor in the young person learning to accept themselves as they are. The love of Jesus is very powerful and it can lead us to trust in situations where we feel very isolated and helpless. But it is also true to say that Jesus is uniquely placed to help the young person, for by his death and resurrection there is hope of new life. A glimpse of this kind of hope, even in the middle of much darkness, can be a lifeline for a young person suffering from an eating disorder. One of the songs written by the young people here in Oxford says this much better than I can:

> I turned my back on the Love of the Lord,
> Turned my back on his light,
> But walking around in the depths of the dark,
> Maybe his love was right.
>
> So I'm walking away from the shadows,
> I'm walking out of the rain,
> I'm walking out of these dark caves,
> And into his sunshine again,
> I'm spinning around in his glory,
> I'm moving away from the pain,
> I'm climbing out of the darkness,
> And into his arms again.
>
> I can only stumble around in the dark,
> In the light it is safe to run free,
> So I'm reaching out for his unseen hand,
> Knowing if I fall, that he'll catch me.[3]

The cross is also about the victory Christ has won for us over evil. I feel very strongly that eating disorders are best explained in terms of the bondage which traps young girls into a destructive cycle; this to me is evil – I don't mean in the sense of a personal demon or devil, although I do believe in these. I have heard of some girls who personify their eating disorder as some kind of demon which is attacking them.

Having said this though, I'm talking here more about a sense of being trapped by a force which is hard to shake off. In these circumstances the death and resurrection of Jesus can be talked about as the power of victory over evil. For this reason the love of Jesus and his call to step into the light is made possible for us, but it should never be seen as a substitute for proper medical care, rather, a parallel and supplement to it.

Escape

Most young people at one time or another experiment with soft drugs and with alcohol. Most concerned adults get very worried for young people when they realize this kind of behaviour is taking place. In my experience, getting worked up about all of this doesn't help much. Of course, some drugs are extremely harmful, but we need to treat this matter with a measure of perspective if we are going to be of any help to young people. Very often, given a bit of space they will work out for themselves that the abuse of alcohol and drugs is not what it's cracked up to be.

However, some young people do have very destructive relationships with drugs and alcohol. Some young people find in drugs and alcohol a way to escape from their problems. Getting high or drunk can be one way to avoid facing up to the uncomfortable realities of life. Of course we all do this to some extent. When I read a novel or watch a film I am escaping into another world, but I am only doing this so that I can eventually go back and face my life refreshed and relaxed. For many young people this sense of balance between escape and responsibility has been eroded, and in some cases it has never been learned.

For those who take drugs the experience they get can become a much more attractive place than their school or their home. This sort of retreat into a more comfortable and rewarding world is in reality a permanent holiday. The illegality of taking drugs creates a kind of fellowship for those who are in on the scene and this just tends to emphasize the escape which is taking place. In this way most young people become hooked on drugs in a psychological rather than a physical sense.

In trying to help these kinds of young people, focusing on the habit of taking drugs is usually a mistake, since this is the symptom and not the cause of their problems. It is always much better to try to look for what it is they are trying to escape from. In most cases this will be some sort of conflict or tension in their lives – the pressure of school work, the fear of the future, or stress at home. As a friend it is important that we are able to care for these young people in a way which does not condemn them or treat them as some kind of social leper. Rather, there is a need to find ways to support the young person as (s)he tries to face up to whatever it is that (s)he is running away from. This does not mean that we should condone drug taking or abuse of alcohol; it simply means we start with the needs of the person themselves.

One area I think is very helpful in relation to alcohol is if young people are able to see people using it in a responsible way. This is one reason why I would be willing to meet young people "down the pub". If they see that I am able to drink in a controlled way, this gives them a positive role model to follow. The same holds true where young people come round to my house for a meal where alcohol might be available. But these sorts of things are no real substitute for talking through the problems and conflicts that might be behind the young person's drug-taking or abuse of alcohol.

Helping young people to see their problems clearly and then make a plan to sort things out can be a very rewarding experience. It might well be that taking an hour or two to listen to what is going on in the young person's life will help to get the thing straight in their head. In other situations they may need to be helped to see what is going on by questions which allow them the space to explore the issue. Again Jesus as a friend and guide has much to commend itself in this situation. Many young people will be very willing to accept this kind of help within a Christian framework. If they have come up with a particularly knotty problem you might feel free to say that in a similar situation you would ask God to help you sort it out. You might make it clear that you will be praying for guidance to help you to see clearly what is going on. Where friendship has been built up over some time the young person will most probably accept this as being a genuine part of your life and they will welcome your concern. But whatever approach you adopt the emphasis should make clear that taking drugs and abusing alcohol is only a symptom of their problems, however worrying these habits may be. If the young person can be helped to turn and face their problems then there is a sense in which true repentance has taken place for in the Bible repentance is seen as a turning from darkness to life.

Responsibility

One of the big problems about being an adult is that people expect you to be responsible. Being "responsible" can cover so many different areas of your life – you are expected to be responsible as a driver, responsible with money, responsible in your sex life. In fact, being an adult is quite a feat! It's no wonder then that teenagers find the transition from being a child, where little is expected of them in terms of responsibility, to being an adult laden down with so many "responsibilities" very difficult indeed.

The pattern for most young people is that they learn what it means to be responsible over a period of time. From the outside their learning process can look very alarming. Many a youth group has started off with strong and seemingly very able leadership from "older young people" which has descended into chaos within a month or two. Young people who were at first very keen to help out find the "responsibility" of the whole thing too much to bear over a period of time. All of this is very natural and our role as friends and youthworkers is to help each young person as they struggle to become an adult, and then be around to ensure a major disaster does not occur when it goes wrong.

However, for some young people this safety net of adults or parents who can sort things out and then give them another chance at a later date, is not a help. Family tension and break-up can often mean that teenagers have to take on "responsibility" sooner than they can possibly handle it. I know of one young person who was made homeless by his father at 15 years of age. Suddenly he had to find a flat, visit the benefit office, fill in forms, look for a job he could do, and try to finish off at school. He told me once, "I'm facing problems I'm too young to be dealing with." Of course he was right.

A good many young people are thrown out of the house at some time or another, while others walk out in a fit of rage. But however the situation has come about suddenly they face a whole new set of very complex problems. On one side will be the tensions and problems with their family, which will mean they are in a pretty upset state anyway. But if they are going to live apart from their family, or if they are forced to do so, then their problems represent a massive mountain which they will almost certainly not climb without the odd fall.

Most young people who find themselves without a home do have certain support networks which they can draw on. Friends will very often put them up for the night and those friends often have parents who can offer food and advice. It is quite possible that a teenager can exist on friends' settees and floors for quite some time. Staying with friends in this way is very important but after a while it is just one way of escaping "responsibility" for what has gone on. The homeless teenager will either have to go and talk to his/her parents, or else will have to find somewhere to live. This decision will not go away even if you ignore it or block it out with drink, it is a very uncomfortable reality to face.

It is not uncommon for a teenager in this sort of situation to need some sort of a shock to get them going on the problem. For one young person I knew, a couple of nights sleeping rough made them decide to sort out their problems. Within a few days they had sorted out a flat, got a deposit together and moved in with a promise of money from housing benefit, and a job offer in the pipeline. For others the agony is much more drawn out.

The odds are stacked against any young person who has not got either somewhere to live or a job; for without one of these two you are in serious trouble. Without a job you can't get a deposit together for a flat, and without an address you can't get a job. Being homeless means that just surviving becomes an all-consuming business – but this is not all. Within a short time of being homeless a young person begins to lose their sense of value and self-worth. These two factors together mean that it is very hard indeed for a homeless young person to start to break out of the poverty trap they are in. In these circumstances some form of hostel or shelter is a vital lifeline which can offer a place of safety and security where young people can sort things out.

My own experience of homelessness amongst young people has so far been with those who for a brief period have fallen out with their parents and been kicked out of their homes. What follows is based largely on that experience. These young people are fortunate in that they have their own friendship networks and families to fall back on. Young people who move away from their home town to one of the big cities are, I realize, in a much more desperate situation.[4] For some I have known, the problems they face become too much for them and a cycle of partial success and irresponsibility sets in. They get a job and then a flat, but they fail to pay the rent and so after three months they get thrown out. They get a flat, but they lose their job and so go on housing benefit, but one month they spend it all down at the pub and once again they get thrown out of their flat. The cycle repeats itself in a young person's life simply because they find it so hard to take on fully what it means to be an adult and therefore responsible.

On the face of it there would seem to be a great deal an adult friend could do to help a young person who has become homeless in these kinds of circumstances. In the first place there is the offer of a meal, a bed for the night and somewhere to leave their stuff during the day. But there needs to be a word of caution here. Most young people, given a kind adult and a warm place to stay, will use this as an excuse not to face up to what they must do. As an adult involved with a homeless young person there is a very delicate path to tread between a lack of care and too much care. I have always tried in these sorts of situations to set very clear limits on how long a young person can stay in my house. Normally this will be for one night or over the weekend, but I make it clear that I am setting this limit because I want them eventually to go to the relevant people, i.e. parents, DSS, county council, landlords. Usually I will not go to these people with a young person, or phone up on their behalf, or do anything which takes the initiative away from the young person themselves. However, I make it clear that I am always available to talk through the decisions they are making and as the whole process starts to proceed I become more willing to help out. This probably sounds very hard, and I must admit sometimes I have got the balance wrong, but it is vital that young people take responsibility for their own lives.

Responsibility is displayed in the toughest of circumstances when Jesus died for the sins of the world on the cross. This act of obedience on his part has always been an inspiration to Christian people to turn and face life in obedience to God. Jesus's death renews our resolve to get down to the nitty-gritty of life. I know one young person who continually faced the kinds of problems I have talked about in this chapter, and to him Jesus was exactly this kind of example. When life got tough he would turn to Jesus and draw strength to struggle on, and when he messed things up he knew he had let Jesus down as well because he knew Jesus was calling him to be responsible. He drew inspiration from a song he had on a cassette, and in times of trouble he talked of this song as his Bible.

> Where does it all lead?
> Which turning do we take?
> Feelings left behind,
> There's far too much at stake.
>
> But the vision grows stronger every day
> And the mist has clouded the way.
> Do we leave tomorrow or do we stay?
> And will we ever have our say?
>
> Seems useless to go on,
> Directions are all blurred
> Life is never easy
> But something needs to stir.

I want to carry on
'Cause the vision doesn't change.
But if you've lost your way
There's time to rearrange.[5]

NOTES

1. Kubler-Ross: *On Death and Dying*.
2. Material supplied by Sam Adams and Tess Ward.
3. Oxford Youth Works, Copyright Sea Dream Music, 1991.
4. For help in this area see Logan: *A Life to be Lived*.
5. "Visions Never Sleep", Simon Law, Copyright Sea Dream Music.

PART IV

*

So What?

13

True Disciples

Following Jesus is always a tough challenge. Not only do you have to be continually in touch with Jesus in prayer, worship and Bible study, but you also have to work out what it is that he wants you to do in life. For those of us growing up within the Church, or those of us who have grown up in a conformist middle-class family, the task of discipleship is made easier by the mere fact that so many people have gone before us and trailblazed what it means to be a Christian within a middle-class context. Through their struggles and problems they have hammered out patterns of discipleship.

Patterns of discipleship

Christian nurture within our churches is by and large built upon already-established patterns of Christian living. A new convert coming into the Church models his or her Christian life upon the people around them who are older Christians. Sometimes this modelling takes place in a much more formal environment such as a Sunday school, youth group or a fellowship group. But wherever people learn what it means to be a Christian, the basic cultural setting will nearly always assume middle-class values and life style. In other words, patterns of discipleship taught within our existing church set-ups are designed within, and, therefore, only work for people willing to accept, the conformist middle-class way of life.

I spoke to one young Christian who regularly used a set of Bible reading notes. He complained that they were unrealistic when you tried to do the things they suggested in the inner city where he lived. He told me about one set of notes that suggested you tried smiling at everyone you met that day. He told me how he came out of his flat onto a busy road first thing in the morning, and by the time he had walked fifteen yards about two hundred people had passed him all rushing to get to work, so how on earth was he going to smile at all of them?! The problem was that the Bible reading notes assumed a certain way of life and wrote about how to try to be Christian in that context, and for my friend, who lived in a totally different world, they simply did not work.

For those young people outside the middle-class world of the Church, following Jesus becomes a very complicated procedure. When a working-class young person becomes a Christian it is not uncommon for them to start to lose contact with their background. This is, of course, not the specific aim of any Church; however, the problem lies within what is accepted as the pattern of discipleship. If a young person is only able to see a middle-class form of Christian discipleship then (s)he will nearly always follow that pattern.

Friendship and discipleship

Going to meet young people on their home territory as friends is a vital way to start to form new patterns of Christian discipleship. In the first place the relevance of Jesus to the situation of the young people is demonstrated in very concrete and practical ways of caring. Since actions speak louder than words this part of our witness should never be underrated. Young people will use our way of living as a pattern for their own discipleship.

But there are also the many discussions that arise out of the problems the young people themselves are dealing with. Here again an adult friend can encourage the young person to work out what it means to be a Christian within their own cultural setting. But all of these ways of forming new patterns of Christian discipleship will need to be undertaken within the basic friendship group which the young people themselves have already formed.

In our own work in Oxford we have concentrated on forming discipleship groups out of already-existing friendship networks. So if we are in contact with a group of working-class young people then we will endeavour to work through the question of Christian commitment with the group as a whole, rather than direct individuals to various youth groups and churches as soon as they become interested in becoming Christians.

This approach has a number of advantages:

1. There are a number of issues to do with life style which do not have any bearing on the Christian faith, but which are very important to young people. For instance, a large number of young people will feel much happier talking about personal issues in a place where they can smoke. Working with their own group this is less of a problem than trying to get a church youth group to accept this habit. The same goes for swearing; most young people will use swear words as a usual way to express their feelings. In a church setting this would be considered to be unacceptable, but within their own group they can feel free to express their faith in any way they wish to.

2. Swearing is not the only issue related to language which makes an established friendship group the best place to talk about discipleship. The words we use to express our experience of God are very important. These words go some way to shape our understanding of God as well as help us to work out what it means to live a Christian life. It is vital that young people are able to form their own characteristic expression of faith and to do this they must create their own religious language. In their own friendship groups this process can take place in a much more natural way than if they were to be introduced to the predominantly middle-class way of talking about God which we have in our churches. It is very easy for a young person who has newly come to faith to simply adopt the jargon associated with our Christian youth groups. If they are encouraged to try to express their experience of God in their own words then it is much more likely they will find words and expressions which resonate with a more genuine impact in their own lives and culture.

3. If Christian discipleship is worked through with a group of young people who come from the same background then it is much more likely they will continue in their faith as they grow older. One of the biggest problems for young people who step outside their cultural framework in order to find faith in Christ is that they become alienated from their friends and family. By working with a group of young people this problem can be largely eliminated, because the whole group can support each other in their faith. They see each other in school and on the street corner, so as problems arise they can be of help to each other.

4. The most important reason for working with a group of young people on the problems of Christian discipleship is that they know more about their culture than I, as an adult, do. There is a sense in which as adults we are trying to help young people to make steps along a path we may never have been along. As Christian adults we may have very little idea of the problems and tensions that being a Christian will involve for the young people we have come to know. In many cases we will not even know the questions, let alone the answers, that will come out of an attempt to live a Christian life within their culture. Moreover, there are large groups of people in our country who have never been reached by the Gospel. It is therefore not at all unusual to find that young people know of no one in their family, or even in their area, who has any Christian commitment at all. In this context, living out the Christian faith is a pioneering job and the young people themselves need to act as our guides and instructors. We need to learn from them what the issues are, before we attempt to help with any answers. Friendship groups therefore need to work together to find out how being a Christian can make sense within a particular culture.

5. Working in a group is also very important because young people need the skills and insights of a number of different people as they work out their path of discipleship. We have found that different young people bring a variety of different gifts to a discipleship group – some are good at finding things

out, others know a lot about their area, some can write songs, others like to pray, some are avid readers of the Bible. Together a group can benefit from the gifts and abilities of each other and together they can grow.

Following friendship patterns

In Chapter 6 I explored a number of different friendship patterns. It is very important that any group which meets to discuss Christian discipleship is built upon, and does not fight against, the friendship patterns already established by the young people themselves.

With working-class young people who identify very strongly with a particular area, it is vital that a discipleship group also identifies with that area. We have found that young people who live on the estates round Oxford are much happier meeting on their home territory. In fact, they are very suspicious of anything which is organized in the centre of town or on the other side of town. But there is more to this than simply ensuring the young people come to whatever you are running. There is a sense in which meeting to talk about faith right in the centre of their estate brings Jesus to life for them in that area. You don't meet Jesus only by going somewhere where middle-class people live, Jesus is willing to meet us here. This can cause some problems when you go to a church on the other side of town and you need somewhere to meet with a group of young people.

Again we have found that there is much benefit in trying to form links with local churches on estates, even where these churches are not considered to be very lively. In most cases local clergy have been very open to the sort of friendship outreach that we have adopted, and they are also a possible link in the future when the discipleship group starts to feel the need for a church to belong to.

With more middle-class groups of young people we have found it much easier to use venues for meeting which are more central. With some groups of "rebellious" middle-class young people who are used to getting together in the centre of town or in one of the local pubs it is very easy to start a group in a neutral place. However, if they identify with that place very strongly then it has to be recognized that other more conformist young people may be unwilling to meet there. This can cause big problems if you use your local church hall for a rebellious group who then decide to colonize the place, hanging around on the streets outside and sitting in the church porch. One way round this problem is to use the young peoples' homes. With more conformist groups we have very successfully used their front rooms to hold discussion groups. This can also lead to very fruitful contact with their parents as well as providing a warm and friendly place to meet.

Using our own words in worship

Most young people I have known closely over the last years have been interested in playing in rock bands. Their style has often been very "alternative" and rebellious, though their musical interest has always led them to a sensitivity for things that are creative and also issues that are more spiritual. Over the last few years a number of these young people have become Christians and it has been very natural for them to start to express their faith in the songs that they write and perform in the local pubs and clubs around Oxford. From the start we tried to encourage this kind of self-expression, so that they could come up with their own words and language for faith. This first started to happen when we got together to write songs for their band and it was a very natural and easy thing for them to try to express our experience of Jesus. This was important for two reasons. First, it allowed the young people to form their own "picture" of Jesus and then, having formed it, they were strengthened in their faith by looking again at that picture. And secondly, they realized that they could use their own words to talk about God, which gave them a sense of importance.

From performing songs in the band we moved to a form of worship. Together we wrote a number of songs which we could sing together "to God", instead of to an audience. Once again it was important that we were using words written by the group itself, but what was even more important was the sense that God found these words acceptable.

So often the Church has been seen by young people to support a reactionary, "adult" view of life. The group of young people I had got to know were acutely aware of the ways that the "Church" fell short of their own values and ideals. However, when we began to worship God together something amazing dawned on us.

I probably need to describe the scene a little bit. We first started meeting in my office, a very small, long, thin room. At one end, crammed up against the desk, we set up a drum kit. The rest of us would squat on the floor up the other end of the room. At first there were only five of us but the small space made us feel very close – in all senses! With a full set of drums and an electric guitar blasting away the noise was pretty deafening, but the young people would pass a microphone round during the songs so that the words could be heard.

The group had a keen sense for the "mystical" in life (it emerged later that many of them were extensively involved in "occult" practices). To fit their sense of the "spiritual" we would draw the curtains and light "candles" around the room. The songs we had written were very simple and we would sing them over and over again, much like a Taizé chant. In fact, the atmosphere was very like a Taizé service, apart from the fact that we played loud music, and also that most of the young people were smoking cigarettes. In between the songs we would keep silence and try to pray in our own way to God. After a while one of us would read from the Bible and we would talk about it.

The first time we met together in this way each of us was struck incredibly powerfully by a sense of the presence of God. This was perhaps the single most important element in everything that has developed since in Oxford. Suddenly the young people realized that God could take their songs, their words, their service, their lives, and could make them his own. Given the largely rebellious and alienated culture of this group this acceptance by God was very powerful. Suddenly they realized that Jesus was willing to meet them where they were at, within their culture. Their words and their music could become a place where God would visit them. This was pretty mind-blowing – suddenly God was willing to enter their culture and make them his friends.

Since we started our worship time we have been forced to move out of my office so that we could fit the people in. Now we number nearly 30 people each week. Our songs have grown with us also, and below are two of the songs we regularly use. The first is called "Love and Fear"; it started life as a song we used to perform in one of the rock bands, and now we use it in our worship. The second is "Is this Believing?", and it was written by one of the young people who has written many of the songs we now sing together.

Love and fear

In spite of all the heartache
You're always there.
A new light to follow,
A new hope to share.

We keep fighting through the years,
Having you means love and fear.

Maybe I'm just shallow
Or maybe I just use you when I'm down,
But I can't help but follow
Whenever you're around.

We keep fighting through the years,
Having you means love and fear.[1]

Is this believing?

You died on a wooden cross,
With thorns on your head,
Nails through your hands and feet,
and a sword in your side.

You tell me you understand,
The thorns in my words,
The nails that still pierce my heart,
And the sword through my soul.

Is this believing?
Or am I dreaming?[2]

Ownership and worship

We very often have people come to visit us at Oxford Youth
Works and more often than not we take them to our worship
time. One common misunderstanding these people have is that
what we are doing is significant because the words of the songs
are "original" or because the "form" our worship takes is
"new" and "exciting". These things may well be true, but this
is not why the young people feel a sense of commitment to the
worship. The most important factor we have come to value
above everything else is that the young people feel this worship
time is "theirs". This is partly a matter of "culture", the service
fits the group's way of behaving very well. But it is also a matter
of "power": the group feels that they own the worship time,
that it belongs to them.

These two factors are vitally important if you are setting out
on your own path with a group of young people. It would be
very wrong to assume that a worship time with young people
writing their own songs is the right thing to do with your local
group. It is essential to start with the friendship patterns and
particular culture of the group that you have got to know. Start
with the young people themselves and not with the latest bright
idea from the Christian world because this ensures that the
group takes part in creating whatever comes about. If they are
involved from the start then they will feel that it is "theirs".
This also ensures that the issues the group deals with, and the
way in which these issues are expressed, will grow from their
world, and therefore have much more power within that
world. True disciples are not only true to Christ, they must also
be true to their own culture.

NOTES

1. "Love and Fear", Copyright Sea Dream Music.
2. "Is this Believing?", Rozz MacDonald, Copyright Sea Dream Music.

14

Reading the Bible

Almost every movement which has brought about the growth and renewal of the Church has started with people reading the Bible and seeing in its message a new relevance to their lives. If young people are going to be successful in finding new ways to live as Christian disciples within their own culture, then they must start by being able to read and understand the Bible. They have to be able to read about Jesus for themselves; for only as they read his words and hear about the things he did, will they be equipped to follow him. At the beginning an adult Christian friend will start by telling young people about Jesus and how he could become real in their lives. But this relationship should not be continued for too long after the young people have decided to follow Jesus. As soon as possible they need to be encouraged to tackle the Bible for themselves and on their own. However, there are a number of problems to be overcome if young people are going to be free in their interpretation of the Bible.

Won't read can't read

Large numbers of young people find reading very difficult. In some cases this is because they have never learned to read; in others it is simply the fact that they have never been in the habit of reading. These problems are not at all unusual – in fact, an aversion to reading is very normal amongst young people. However there are ways to work around this sort of cultural block.

1. *Working in groups:* We have found that young people will think about the Bible and its message very happily in a group

context, whereas they may never get around to reading the Bible on their own. Usually we write the Bible passage on a small bit of paper. Somehow a small paragraph on a page can be easier to digest than something which comes out of a book. We normally work on the Bible in groups of four or five and we give each group the bit of paper, and the instructions to one of the young people. If adults sit in on a group they are told not to act as leader or as the fount of all wisdom.

2. *Making it concrete:* Most Bible studies work on the basic idea that you are trying to "understand" the ideas in the Bible. By understand, they mean wrestle with the Bible message at the level of ideas and concepts. This approach works well for university-type people who are most happy with theory. However, most people like to know about how things work out in practice. Take the example of a piece of machinery, such as a vacuum cleaner that has gone wrong. From diagrams and books it is possible to sort out what might have happened, but most people will need to get their hands on the machine and "see" how each part moves and relates to the others before they are able to work out how to fix it. In this case, understanding is a very practical, experience-based process. The same sort of approach needs to be used when young people read the Bible.

One way of working with the Bible in a more practical way is to get a group to act out a Bible story. Most often the Bible story will be "up-dated" so that particular characters in the Bible become modern-day equivalents. This sort of exercise has two effects. The first is that the relevance of a Bible passage is seen much more clearly by it being brought into a present-day setting, but there is also the fact that the young people actually "experience" what it is like to be a part of the Bible story. If we take the story of the Good Samaritan (always a favourite because it has a good bit of violence at the start), each person in the story will be able to say how they are feeling and why they think they are doing what they are doing. In this way the experience of doing the Gospel story can be explored with a group and made to be as relevant as possible.

3. *Seeing the parallels:* Another way to try to make the Bible

come alive to young people is to get them to draw specific parallels between Bible characters and stories and people that they know in life. Last Christmas we all did this kind of exercise in small groups and then we shared our results with each other. We decided that if Jesus came today then the shepherds would be people from the local Rover Works on night shift and the three wise men would be astronomer Patrick Moore, so that he could follow the star, historian and "Mastermind" anchorman Magnus Magnusson and TV journalist Kate Adie.

All of this might sound a bit of a lark, and to be honest it was, but there was a serious attempt to try to make sense of the Bible story in a way which impacted on the world which the young people were familiar with.

4. *Telling stories:* Reading a Bible story out loud can be very dull for most young people. So, if it is at all possible, we try to re-tell the Bible story in our own words. This way the flow of events can be given a more dramatic feel. Usually there is very little need for any change to the Bible stories, it is just that the odd details can be given a bit more weight if you tell the story yourself. I still remember one teenager telling the story of Peter walking on the water; he stood in the middle of the room and swayed with every gust of wind and rocked with every wave, until suddenly he began to sink into the sea. This fine story was told using vivid words and actions and it served to bring this event to life.

Young people who find reading difficult can take these kind of stories and interpret them in their own way. One other way to use the Bible in a story form is to simply read to a group the Bible passage but try to do it in a way which gives the events life and energy.

One result of using the power of the Bible as a story is that young people find that they are drawn into the events and the characters. A story affects people at more than a purely rational level, it also affects how we feel.

5. *Working from experience:* One way to encourage young people to read the Bible is to show how something they have

experienced is exactly the same as something they can read about in the Bible.

Every year we take a group of young people away for a week's holiday. We always mix the types of young people on what we have called our "camp", although we don't use tents, I assure you! Here is what one young person wrote after coming on this camp:

"I remember returning from my first camp feeling that my thoughts about other people would never be the same. Before the camp I used to look at a Gothic and think 'what a wanker'. A Gothic was someone to be laughed at and not spoken to. That changed in a week. I realized that just because someone looked different didn't mean I couldn't be friends with them. I felt an openness that I had never imagined to be in me, and with that openness came a respect from my peers. The fact which astounded me most of all was that the stereotype that Christians are boring is wrong. The complete opposite is true."

This young person had experienced in a very powerful way what Paul was describing in Galatians 3:28: "So there is no difference between Jews and Gentiles, slaves and free men, between men and women; you are all one in Christ Jesus." After the camp had happened it would be much easier to talk about the unity Jesus brings between different types of people, because I could say, "Remember what happened on camp? Well it is exactly like that when Jesus starts to bring people together." Working from experience to the Bible in this way can be very powerful, because suddenly the reality of the biblical message is demonstrated in a simple, yet appropriate way.

Sometimes young people can use their experience of life to open up the biblical message in quite unexpected ways. I remember one Bible study with a group of young people who had been very deeply involved in the occult. For these young people the experience of demon possession and oppression by spiritual powers was much more real in their lives than it has ever, thankfully, been in mine. Reading about the temptation of Jesus by Satan in the wilderness with these young people drew many parallels with their own lives. Evil and temptation were very big issues for them and the power of their past occult activities was still casting a long shadow across their lives. But the victory of Jesus over Satan in the wilderness was a great comfort to them. If Jesus could win over temptation then so could they. Much occult practice is to do with the exercise of power and influence. The group were very quick to point out that each of the temptations centres around the correct and the wrong use of spiritual power and influence. Jesus, however, was able to see the right use of his position as the Son of God and he sent Satan on his way. It was helpful to these young people that Jesus had this clarity of vision, for it gave them hope in their own situation.

6. *Translating the Bible:* One really good way to help young people make sense of the Bible is to ask them to read a passage and translate what it says into their own words. I tried this out with a good friend of mine called Keith. One day Keith and I were reading Psalm 23 in a Bible study group. I had read this famous part of the Bible out loud to the group, but Keith couldn't really make any sense of it. So we decided to take the psalm line by line and translate it into more down-to-earth language. I read out each verse and Keith would put it into terms which made sense to him:

Keith on Psalm 23

Jesus guides me, 'cos shepherds guide sheep.
He helps me if I'm in a tight spot.

He gives me time out to get myself together.
If I make a mistake I'm not gonna get butchered over it.
He gives me a new start,
Without
reminding me of what I've done wrong.

I've got new hope as he pushes me towards
the right path and he's always with me.

Through the grief of life I don't have to worry 'cos
Jesus is with me telling me that it's not the end
of the world.

Jesus has set up a dinner for me where people that
hate me look at me and see that Jesus is treating
me better and not less than anyone else.

As long as I live he will still be there for me.
I'm always welcome wherever he is.
Even if I do screw up, he'll still be waiting.

Here Keith is putting this famous psalm into his own words.
The result is that suddenly this passage takes on a new and
relevant meaning. The words have a bite about them and also a
particular application. This, of course, isn't a translation for
universal use, although "The Bible According to Keith" has a
nice ring to it! Keith is here making sense of this psalm for
himself. What was interesting about this exercise was that after
we had completed the whole psalm we looked at the
"translation" and it suddenly came alive to us both in a totally
new way. Keith was rightfully very pleased with his translation
and it inspired him to go back to the Bible and study some of
the other psalms for himself.

One further point which I began to realize when I looked at
the completed psalm in Keith's translation was that the
language used in most translations of the Bible is quite some
way away from the language used by the average teenager. In
preparing this version of the psalm with Keith I used the Good
News Version, a translation which is meant to communicate
with a limited vocabulary and in common speech. If you
compare the Good News text of Psalm 23 with Keith's version
you'll see how far short of these aims it falls.

7. *Meditating on the Word:* The words of the Bible can often
stir young people to prayer and a love of God. One way I have
found to be very effective, especially in our worship times, has
been to read a Bible passage to a group of young people who

are sitting in silence or with their eyes closed. Usually I have asked the group to be willing to be open to God meeting them in and through the words of the passage, and to do this they don't have to try to understand every word. In fact, it is better if they just let the words wash over them and if a phrase or an image strikes them as being very relevant they should feel free to let it stay in their mind. One passage I particularly like for this sort of meditation is Isaiah 55:1-11.

We have also experimented with other ways of meditating on the Bible. One very successful exercise is reading a Bible story once, then working slowly through the story again, asking the young people to think themselves into it. A good story for this is the healing of blind Bartimaeus in Mark 10:46-52. You can ask the young people to imagine what it was like in that village – was it hot, was the road sandy or made of dirt? Then imagine they are blind Bartimaeus – how did it feel to be blind, imagine calling out to Jesus, "Take pity on me", think about why you are calling out to Jesus, what do you hope will happen, how do you feel when the people tell you to shut up, what are they afraid of?

This sort of meditation is very powerful, and is a way that young people who might not read a story like this with much interest can become personally involved. By leading a group through this kind of experience the Good News of Jesus can become very real in their lives. However, it is usually a good idea to allow some time for the group to begin to move from meditation back to real life and some sensitivity is needed with this. It can be useful to try to unpack their experience by getting them to share with each other what they felt at each stage of the story. This sort of discussion means the group can learn from each other, and they can also process the experience into their own lives in a more concrete way.

8. *Interpreting the Bible in a context of rebellion:* The Bible is full of material which can make sense to young people who feel very alienated from society. Rebellious young people will see in it much which will reinforce their own criticism of the world. The insights of these kinds of young people are very valuable

because they bring out of the Bible the echo of many things that those of us in the more comfortable middle-class Church fail to see. One very fine example of this can be seen from the Bible studies recorded by Ernesto Cardenal in *The Gospel in Solentiname*. Ernesto was a Catholic who went to minister amongst a group of Nicaraguan peasants in the remote area of Solentiname. He tells in his book how the local people would read a portion of the Gospel every week in their daily service and instead of a sermon they would discuss what the passage had to say to them. Most of the people taking part in these discussions had no education and only a couple of them could read; however, their experience of life included the revolutionary thinking which eventually overthrew the right-wing Samosa regime. In this atmosphere, a number of the young people who were particularly drawn to the Sandinistas would see in the Bible a reflection of their own struggles. Ernesto Cardenal kept a record of these Bible studies. Here is an extract from one of the discussions about Luke 2:41–52, the child Jesus in the temple:

"The young people began to talk. First Manuel: 'He disobeyed. He gave them the slip. And young people should disobey when their parents want to keep them just for themselves, when they want to take them away from the community, from their work with other young people, from their duty, from the struggle.'

"Afterwards, Laureano, who always talks about revolution: 'Like the guerilla fighters who go off to fight against the wishes of their parents.'

"And one of the old men: 'Was it right for a child to do that? Shouldn't he have asked permission first? They wouldn't have refused it. Imagine how worried they felt as they went around looking for him. Mary scolded him . . .'

"And another one of the young people: 'Maybe they wouldn't have given him permission. And that's why he had to do it that way. Jesus here gives us a lesson about independence from the family'"[1]

What is remarkable about this dialogue is the way these people move so freely from the Bible passage to their own situation. With revolution in the air the young people see in Jesus a rebellious youth who has something to say to the older generation. Their understanding of life and the issues they face every day gives them a "framework" to read this story of Jesus. The older people are more cautious, but the result is a discussion about Jesus in the light of the most important issues of the day. This openness to the Bible and to what is actually happening in the life of their country is very refreshing and it brings the Bible alive to speak again to them all.

When young people come to study the Bible we need to allow them the space to explore these kinds of rebellious issues, and their insights on the life of Jesus need to be taken seriously because they will often direct us to real-life problems which we so often neatly side-step in the normal run of things.

The Bible and revolution

The Bible is a very dangerous book. It is not for nothing that throughout history people in power have tried to stop ordinary people reading and interpreting the Bible for themselves. In our own society we don't prohibit people from owning or reading the Bible; however, there is still a great fear of allowing people to think about it in disturbing or rebellious ways. We have produced Bible notes, we have standard and safe commentaries, we ensure that Bible study groups have some kind of guidance and we look to established and safe experts to keep us on the straight and narrow. Theological study is another way that we have wrapped the Bible up in a complicated set of studies which just serves to prove to us how the ordinary person in the street can never really claim to know what the Bible says unless they have done three or four years of intensive study.

All of this is to a large extent the tyranny of the expert and it goes against the spirit of the Christian faith. Young people need to be allowed to read and interpret the Bible without the heavy and restrictive weight of all these so-called "experts". Of course there are problems in ignoring all that has gone before in the Christian tradition, but it is precisely at this point that the youthworker or adult friend has a role to play.

Young people need to be allowed the freedom to explore the faith for themselves, but they will need help and guidance as they do this. This kind of help needs to be offered sensitively and with a large dollop of humility. As adult friends and guides we need to have an eye on the whole of the Christian tradition to see if there is anything which can help the young people as they form their ideas about God from the Bible. Sometimes this may be direction to other parts of the Bible which provide a more balanced picture to work from. Perhaps there will be a need to say what the biblical context actually was to correct a misunderstanding which is taking the group off-course. At other times there will be a particular insight in some of the more authoritative works of Christian doctrine or theology which could provide basic tramlines along which the young people could travel.

In this context it can also be very fruitful to introduce the young people to older people from some of the local churches who can act as spiritual guides and directors. But whatever happens, there should always be the freedom for the young people to seek the word of God for themselves in the Bible. All of this should be done in the confidence that the Holy Spirit will lead them "in to all truth".

NOTES

1. Cardenal: *The Gospel in Solentiname Vol. 1*, pp. 95–96.

15

Relating to the Church

If you put into practice everything I have been saying in this book then I can guarantee that you will run into problems! These problems will cluster around the way that your friendship with young people relates to the existing Church. It's only fair to say that these problems are an inevitable result of going outside of the Church's normal cultural atmosphere to picture Jesus within the culture of young people.

After we had been meeting for some months to worship with young people, in the way I have described already, some of the local ministers started to get concerned. They wanted to know if we were setting up a separate church, and if we didn't intend to be a "church" then when would we get the young people along to their services on a Sunday? So we made particular efforts to invite the group to services. The problem was they didn't like what they saw at church. In fact, they found some of it very difficult to stomach. The question we had to face was what should we do? What follows is some of our thinking which grew out of this situation:

A Youth Church?

With a group of young people who were starting to express their faith in ways relevant to their culture it was obvious that we needed to keep a certain amount of distance from the regular Church.

There is a parallel here between the feminist movement in the Church and our own situation. Many Christian women who have been influenced by the feminist movement feel they need to have "space" to develop a spirituality which reflects their view of life. In a male-dominated Church they need to meet on their own, simply so that they can find the right words to express their experience of God. These new words could form the basis of liturgy, but they could also become what Rosemary Radford Reuther calls "a critical culture". If women are really to make a difference in the church they belong to then they need to begin to find ways of analysing the Church and criticizing it from their "feminist" perspective. They need to do this without men being present – at least in the initial stages.

The same is true for young people who have met Jesus within their own culture. There is a need for these young people to have the "space" to create their own words for talking about God and their own forms of worship, prayer, fellowship, and service.

To those of us brought up in the Church all of this sounds very alarming. In our view the best thing that can happen is that as many different people as possible are united in the Church. By "united in the church" what we usually mean is that they sit in the same room for the same amount of time, singing the same songs. The problem with this approach to "Church" is that it doesn't seem too much different from the roll call in a prisoner-of-war camp! There is a strong suspicion that we are only there to be counted!

One common way we in the Church deal with rebellious groups is by giving them a choice – either fit in with our church, or get out. This kind of thing can be said very quietly, simply by how people act, but sometimes it can be said with some feeling. In the case of our young people this kind of stance by the Church will perhaps push us towards a youth Church. This seems to be a bad idea.

One of the problems with setting up a church around a youth subculture is that everyone in that church will eventually grow up. In other words, the very basis of the church would very quickly lose its point, because people don't stay teenagers for ever (or at least most of us don't). As we have seen earlier, in actual fact young people want to relate to adults and to be accepted by them. This holds good for a church based around a community with a variety of age groups involved, but it doesn't help the concept of a "youth Church". Finally, a short glance at church history will tell us that there has always been a tension between the "institution" of the Church and the small community- or "charismatic"-based groups that spring up from time to time. Where the small "charismatic" groups have separated from the institution they have usually become more rigid and authoritarian than the original Church ever was. In working with young people we were seeking to increase freedom not create more bondage, and a youth Church looked a poor option.

Separate and subversive

One thing seemed pretty clear with our small group meeting to worship. The first thing was that in one sense we were already "Church". I've deliberately avoided saying "a church" or "the Church" by saying "Church". What I mean here is we realized that simply by being a group of Christians we were united to all other Christians, we were part of Christ, and therefore part of his people – the Church.

I went with one of our young people to a church-based event the other day. He was making fun of how the people there were dressed and how they behaved. I turned round and said to him, "Don't make too much fun of them 'cos you're going to spend an awful long time in heaven with them!". He grinned as if to admit that I had a point, but the same thing is also true the other way around. Those of us who go regularly to church will need to face up to the fact that we are linked with all sorts of groups and people we don't like or approve of, because, despite our petty differences, God likes all of us!

The problem is that, even though the young people we knew were, by their relationship with Christ, already a part of the people of God, this fact needed to be expressed in some way. Somewhere along the line the young people in our group will need to go to church. They don't, of course, have to fit in, or conform, but they need to express their membership in a real way.

Being part of a church is a complicated business. We are all looking for so many different things from our church – some want a sense of fellowship, others a sense of spiritual direction and service, some teaching and preaching, others a place to belong and for many a place to worship God. What became clear to us was that a number of these functions were already being provided by our own nurture groups and worship. In fact, because of our separate existence we could be much more responsive to the culture of these young people than the Church, which has to cater for everyone, could ever be. We had a time to worship God, a time of fellowship and a sense of belonging to each other; we had teaching and discussion, and we already had a sense of mission and direction. So what could the Church offer us?

Going to church

Church actually has one or two things going for it. The first is that it has tradition, which is a strength. Young people often want to get the feeling that they have been in a "Church" place. When we have taken young people to more "chorus"-based events, or healing services, they have often reacted negatively. They feel our worship service is like that and so they want something different. In truth, what they want is to go to church.

With one small group of young people we have been attending some of the local church services. We have found that the more preaching-based services designed with students in mind, in Oxford city centre, work fairly well with young people who are naturally a bit academic. But for the rest it's best to find something different. The most important factor is the length of the service; it has to be short! In fact, the shorter the better. Next, an old building, if possible. One of the highlights of our worship last year was when we borrowed a local church for a service. We started the worship at around 11 o'clock at night. The young people were really into being in an old building which we lit with only a few candles. Sitting on the floor in the chancel of the darkened church we could feel the size of this old building around us. It was very moving and spiritual. An old building is very important because it gives a sense of tradition.

With another group of young people we have been going to communion services around the city. They like the symbolism of the bread and the wine and they like a simple intimate service. A short sermon shot straight from the hip and a few hymns. This mix, if it lasts no more than one hour, has been very much welcomed by our young people.

Attending services in this way has been very beneficial. In the first place, the young people feel they are part of the Church. And secondly, the Church sees that they intend to be part of the set-up and yet at the same time there is the freedom for us to explore a variety in our worship which we could never do in a regular church service. In recent months a few of our young people have made formal steps of commitment to these churches by being baptized and confirmed.

Planning for difference

What is needed in our churches is a new sense of experimentation and freedom. If we really are going to reach out to different kinds of people then we need to allow these people to find the space within our churches to express their faith in their own way. One way of doing this would be to allow all sorts of groups to grow and be set up around some kind of central, short worship service. This way there would be less need to try to please every group. So often by trying to keep everyone happy, we please no one, falling between expectations of each group. But this kind of variety and freedom will inevitably bring with it some problems. Not least amongst these is the question of unity. In what sense could we ever say that we were one with each other, if we all meet in separate groups?

If we admit that it is important for young people to express their faith within their culture then "division" will always be a problem. But this need not be insurmountable. If there are different groups of people connected in a church experimenting with new ways of worship, then the pressure is very much off the one central service. If the young people don't expect to get trendy music, and the whole thing is fairly short, then they will probably stick with it. They will know that the modern stuff happens elsewhere. Similarly with those who feel the need to hear sermons and in-depth teaching on various issues. They need not have to put up with young people getting fed up with it all in the back row of the church if they know their needs are being met elsewhere. In other words, I'm suggesting we take most of the specialist and extremely demanding material out of a normal Sunday service and put it somewhere else. This leaves the central Sunday service as primarily a simple time of worship, preferably based around the Communion.

A young Church

The argument throughout this book has been that we need to see Jesus through the eyes of young people. We need to do this not only for the sake of the young people we meet but also for the continued relevance of the Church. At present we are a largely middle-class Church, though there are a few notable exceptions to this rule, but if we are ever going to break out of our class boundaries then we will need to make changes. These changes will come about as we get in touch with people from other subcultures and groups and the key to these changes must be young people themselves. The Church desperately needs to have this injection of life from outside in order to simply survive into the 90s. The problem with our outreach so often is that we fail to see how much the "culture" of the people that we reach out to has to offer us in the Church.

One remarkable fact about young people is that they are continually being innovative and creative. There is incredible life and energy outside of the Church amongst young people. If we were able to connect with this energy in a deeply "Christian" way, i.e. motivated by the Spirit of God and linked to a new vision of the resurrected Jesus, then new life would be a constant feature of our churches.

The key to this new life must surely be the extent to which we are able to set young people free to be creative in their Christian lives. The first clue to this creativity is to recognize that in the long run we cannot do this sort of thing for young people. We need to begin to be working in co-operation with them to bring about new and creative ways of being the Church together. This, as I have already said, means we have to give them a certain amount of freedom and creative space without forcing them to leave our churches because they are being a bit separated.

The next step we need is to start to learn from the young people and value the things that they are beginning to create. This means that our church leaders need to learn skills of dialogue and flexibility in the face of change. At first young people will speak with a very loud and aggressive voice and we need to allow them the space to make their mark in our church lives. We also need to begin to get different groups together to talk and to begin to understand each other. We will only bridge the divide between different kinds of people on the basis of relationships built on mutual respect and tolerance. The young people themselves cannot be given the responsibility to initiate this because they do not hold the power in our churches. They cannot be expected to make things change in church. The responsibility in the first instance lies with those of us who are regular church-goers and with our church leaders.

Time will play a very important part in this process of change. Young people will need it to develop their distinctive contribution to our church life. As members of the Church our role will be to start to form real, and genuine, relationships with them. It is only out of these kinds of relationships that understanding and patience with each other will grow. A church which is able to form such contacts with young people will be one which is always open to new ways of doing things and seeing things. This approach is essential if we are to see how Jesus will be pictured in a constantly-changing society. The perspective of young people is essential for this because they are the renewing agent that God wishes to use in our Church.

Strategies for change

The likelihood is that it will take time for the Church to take on board this kind of approach to young people. If this is the case it is very probable that we will become quite discouraged in our attempts to maintain good relationships between young people and the existing Church. However, this should not lead us to, in any way, abandon our mission to young people. Our first priority must be to start to reach out to young people within their own cultural setting. Change in the Church will follow if we are able to be patient and if we can demonstrate how essential change needs to be. In a way it is entirely unreasonable of us to expect the Church to change before it can see why that change is necessary. It is also very easy to burn out trying to get the Church to change before it is ready.

The best approach is to start to bring a group of young people together so that they can form a new and exciting way of Christian living based upon their particular subculture. This renewed group will then serve as an example of all of the good things that we could, with this group of young people, offer to the on-going life of the local church. The spiritual life and vibrancy of the group will speak volumes to church leaders and ordinary churchgoers if we resist the temptation to close off our group from all contact with the institution of the Church.

It is our role as youthworkers to ensure that young people start to make significant contact with the Church and demonstrate that they don't intend to separate off. This is why at some stage attending church is important. It shows our intention of remaining part of the institution and it forces the hand of the Church to reckon with this new thing that is happening in their midst!

If all of this sounds a bit political and confrontational then I suppose you are right, but the reason for this is that there is such a desperate need for us to take action to bring about change. When Jesus begins to meet young people in new and exciting ways then we will suddenly see how unjust it is for the Church to ignore this movement of the Spirit of God in its midst. Change will then come because of the attractive nature of God's work amongst young people.

A renewed Church

The vision here is that when Jesus starts to meet young people within their own cultural setting the inevitable result will be a renewed Church. This Church will be a young Church, a Church open to young people and therefore open to a changing society.

In a sense this is where we begin to see the full circle. A young Church will not only find itself renewed with an influx of young people — it will also be renewed by the vision for a changed society which these young people will bring to it. If the Church is to be a continually relevant force in our society, existing not only for itself but also for those at present outside of its scope, then it must not quench the perceptions and sensitivities of those young people who join it. For young people will provide more "social" insights into how the Church can be salt and light in the world.

This is the challenge that looking through the eyes of young people at the Gospel presents to the Church. It is a challenge to begin to see new ways that God wants us to start to be involved in the world. With that sense of purpose there will also come new and exciting ways of worship, prayer and fellowship. However, following the lead of young people will take us to some places where we will feel very uncomfortable. They will introduce us to new ways of looking at our "society" and as a result we will be challenged to get involved in new kinds of Christian service. These insights will grow in an exciting way as young people become our guides in a renewed and uniquely relevant "picture" of Jesus.

The relationship between youth culture and the Gospel is one which is full of much promise. But it also is one which demands a great deal of time and energy if it is to bear fruit in our churches. Reaching out in friendship to young people is a very costly calling. But it is to this calling that I believe God is challenging his Church. This is a challenge which we should not take up for the sake of the Church, but for the sake of the Gospel.

NOTES

1. Ruether: *Women Church*.

OUTRODUCTION

In this book I have tried to share some practical insights into how to reach out in friendship to young people. I realize, however, that this kind of work is not for everyone. But I have to point out that the saying remains true, "the fields are ripe and ready for harvest", and lamentably the labourers are still so few. If you feel that God is calling you to this kind of work I would like to give you some last words of encouragement and advice.

My own experience has been that whenever I have taken the risk to go and meet young people, I have found that God has, in some way, been there before me. I can't explain this entirely but I'm telling you this simply so that you might take heart. One remarkable fact is that I have received so much from young people themselves. Their friendship has been very precious to me and I have to admit that I probably have gained more by being around them than they have from knowing me! Stepping out in faith has, in my life, always had its rewards. So if God is tugging at your heart over this matter then I can only recommend very strongly that it is worth taking the risk.

I would also like to say that I have learned from painful experience that it is essential to do this work in a team. Even if you can only get a few friends to pray with you once in a while, it is always good to share the load. Jesus sent his disciples out in twos and I think he did this for good reason.

Finally, could I say that my colleagues and I at Oxford Youth Works are always ready to help people who want to form friendships with young people in the name of Christ. We run a full-time training course and several short-term courses. Please do get in touch with us if you think we can be of help to you.

You can write to us at this address.

Oxford Youth Works
The Old Mission Hall
57A St Clements
Oxford
OX4 1AG

BIBLIOGRAPHY

Psychology and young people

Peter Bruggen and Charles O'Brian, *Surviving Adolescence*, Faber and Faber 1986

John Buckler, *The Adolescent Years*, Castlemead 1987

John C. Coleman, *The Nature of Adolescence*, Methuen 1980
——, *Relationships in Adolescence*, Routledge and Kegan Paul 1974

Robert Coles, *The Moral Life of Children*, Houghton Mifflin 1986

James Dobson, *Preparing for Adolescence*, Kingsway 1978

David Elkind, *All Grown Up and No Place to Go*, Addison-Wesley 1984

Erik H. Erikson, *Childhood and Society*, Penguin 1950
——, *Young Man Luther*, Norton 1958

James W. Fowler, *Stages of Faith*, Harper and Row 1981

Martin Gold and Elizabeth Douvan, *Adolescent Development*, Allyn and Bacon 1969

Ronald Goldman, *Religious Thinking from Childhood to Adolescence*, Routledge and Kegan Paul 1964

J. A. Hadfield, *Childhood and Adolescence*, Penguin 1962

Elisabeth Kubler-Ross, *On Death and Dying*, Macmillan 1969

Gordon R. Lowe, *The Growth of Personality*, Penguin 1972

Mary McCormack, *The Generation Gap*, Constable 1985

Alistair I. McFadyen, *The Call to Personhood*, Cambridge 1990

Simon Meyerson, *Adolescence and Breakdown*, George Allen & Unwin 1975

Desmond O'Donnell, *Understanding Your Adolescent*, Dominican Publications 1987

Michael Rutter and Henri Giller, *Juvenile Delinquency*, Penguin 1983

Charles M. Shelton, *Adolescent Spirituality*, Loyola University Press 1983

Merton P. Strommen, *Five Cries of Youth*, Harper and Row 1974

James Youniss and Jacqueline Smollar, *Adolescent Relations with Mothers, Fathers and Friends*, Chicago 1985

Sociology and young people

Philippe Aries, *Centuries of Childhood*, Penguin 1965

Reginald W. Bibby and Donald C. Posterski, *The Emerging Generation*, Irwin 1985

Michael Brake, *Comparative Youth Culture*, Routledge and Kegan Paul 1985

Iain Chambers, *Popular Culture*, Methuen 1986

———, *Urban Rhythms*, Methuen 1985

Frank Coffield, Carol Borrill and Sarah Marshall, *Growing up at the Margins*, Open University 1986

Albert K. Cohen, *Delinquent Boys*, Macmillan 1955

Stanley Cohen, *Folk Devils and Moral Panics*, Blackwell 1972, 1980

Paul Corrigan, *Schooling the Smash Street Kids*, Macmillan 1979

Margaret Crompton, *Adolescents and Social Workers*, Heinemann 1982

Andrew Dewdney and Martin Lister, *Youth Culture and Photography*, Macmillan 1988

S. N. Eisenstadt, *From Generation to Generation*, Free Press, New York, 1956

Peter Everett, *You'll Never Be Sixteen Again*, BBC 1986

Simon Frith, *The Sociology of Youth*, Causeway 1984

———, *Sound Effects. Youth Leisure and the Politics of Rock and Roll*, Constable 1983

Stuart Hall and Tony Jefferson, *Resistance through Rituals*, Hutchinson 1975

Dick Hebdige, *Subculture the Meaning of Style*, Methuen 1979

Richard Jenkins, *Lads, Citizens and Ordinary Kids*, Routledge and Kegan Paul 1983

Simon Jones, *Black Culture, White Youth*, Methuen 1988

Tom Kitwood, *Disclosures to a Stranger*, Routledge and Kegan Paul 1980

Peter Marsh, Elizabeth Rosser, Rom Harre, *The Rules of Disorder*, Routledge and Kegan Paul 1978

Angela McRobbie, *Feminism and Youth Culture: from Jackie to Just Seventeen*, Macmillan 1991

Angela McRobbie and Mica Nava, *Gender and Generation*, Macmillan 1984

David Marsland, *Sociological Explorations in the Service of Youth*, National Youth Bureau 1978

Fred Milson, *Youth in a Changing Society*, Routledge and Kegan Paul 1972

John Muncie, *The Trouble with Kids Today*, Hutchinson 1984

Jeff Nuttall, *Bomb Culture*, Paladin 1968

Geoffrey Pearson, *Hooligan: a History of Respectable Fears*, Macmillan 1983

Kenneth Roberts, *Youth and Leisure*, George Allen and Unwin 1983

David Robbins, *We Hate Humans*, Penguin 1984

Theodore Roszak, *The Making of a Counter Culture*, Faber and Faber 1970

Cyril Simmons and Winnie Wade, *I Like to Say What I Think*, Kogan Page 1984

J. C. Walker, *Louts and Legends: Male Youth Culture in an Inner City School*, Allen and Unwin, Australia

David Whittaker, *Youth in Society*, Longman 1984

Paul Willis, *Learning to Labour*, Saxon House 1977

———, *Common Culture*, Open University Press 1990

Theology

Gerald Arbuckle, *Earthing the Gospel*, Geoffrey Chapman 1990

Mortimer Arias, *Announcing the Reign of God*, Fortress 1984

Leonardo Boff, *Ecclesiogenesis*, Collins 1986

Fredrick Buechner and Lee Boltin, *The Faces of Jesus*, Stearn/Harper Row 1989

Ernesto Cardenal, *The Gospel in Solentiname Vols 1–4*, Orbis 1987

James H. Cone, *The Spirituals and the Blues*, Seabury 1972

Orlando E. Costas, *Christ Outside the Gate*, Orbis 1984

Vincent J. Donovan, *Christianity Rediscovered*, SCM Press 1978

Ian M. Fraser, *Reinventing Theology as the People's Work*, Wild Goose 1980, 1988

Laurie Green, *Let's Do Theology*, Mowbray 1990

Sione Amanaki Havea, *South Pacific Theology*, Regnum Books 1987

David J. Hesselgrave, *Communicating Christ Cross-Culturally*, Zondervan 1978

David J. Hesselgrave and Edward Rommen, *Contextualization*, Apollos 1989

Charles H. Kraft, *Christianity in Culture*, Orbis 1984

Charles H. Kraft and Tom N. Wisley, *Readings in Dynamic Indigeneity*, William Carey 1979

Marvin K. Mayers, *Christianity Confronts Culture*, Zondervan 1974

Carlos Mesters, *Defenseless Flower*, Orbis 1989

Lesslie Newbigin, *The Gospel in Pluralist Society*, SPCK 1989

Eugene A. Nida, *Customs, Culture and Christianity*, Tyndale Press 1954

H. Richard Niebuhr, *Christ and Culture*, Harper and Row 1951

Jaroslav Pelikan, *Jesus Through the Centuries*, Yale, 1985

Don Richardson, *Peace Child*, Regal Books 1974

Christopher Rowlands and Mark Corner, *Liberating Exegesis*, SPCK 1990

Rosemary Radford Ruether, *Sexism and God Talk*, SCM Press 1983

———, *Women Church*, Harper and Row 1985

Robert J. Schreiter, *Constructing Local Theologies*, SCM Press 1985

Aylward Shorter, *Toward a Theology of Inculturation*, Geoffrey Chapman 1988

C. S. Song, *Tell Us Our Names*, Orbis 1984
Hans-Ruedi Weber, *On a Friday Noon*, SPCK 1979
Anton Wessels, *Images of Jesus*, SCM Press 1990
Theo Witvliet, *A Place in the Sun*, SCM Press 1985

Youth ministry

Nick Aiken, *Working with Teenagers*, Marshall Pickering 1988
Clive Andrews, *A Handbook of Parish Youth Work*, Mowbray 1984
Mark Ashton, *Christian Youth Work*, Kingsway 1986
John Benington, *Culture, Class and Christian Beliefs*, Scripture Union 1973
Warren S. Benson and Mark H. Senter III, *The Complete Book of Youth Ministry*, Moody Press 1987
Anthony Campolo, *Ideas for Social Action*, Youth Specialties 1983
Steve Chalke, *The Complete Youth Manual Vol. 1*, Kingsway 1987
Les Christie, *Unsung Heroes*, Zondervan 1987
John Coleman and Gregory Baum, *Youth Without a Future?*, Concilium 1985
David Collyer, *Double Zero*, Evesham 1973
Terry Dunnell, *Mission and Young People at Risk*, Frontier Youth Trust 1985
Michael Eastman, *Inside Out*, Falcon 1976
John Eddison, *Bash: A Study in Spiritual Power*, Marshalls 1982
R. M. Enroth, E. E. Ericson, C. B. Peters, *The Story of the Jesus People*, Paternoster 1972
Mike Fearon, *With God on the Frontiers*, Scripture Union 1988
John Fethney, *Options for Youth*, Angel Press 1985
Steve Flashman, *Closing the Gap*, Kingsway 1988
Leslie J. Francis, *Teenagers and the Church*, Collins 1982
——, *Rural Anglicanism*, Collins 1985
Ian Green and Brian Hewitt, *Collected Wisdom for Youth Workers*, Marshall Pickering 1988

John Halliburton, *Educating Rachel*, SPCK 1987

David and Jean Hewitt, George Burton, *A Study in Contradictions*, Hodder and Stoughton 1969

Bob Holman, *Kids at the Door*, Blackwell 1981

Paul Hooper, *Being Young in an Old Church*, Grove 1986

Douglas Johnson, *Contending for the Faith*, IVP 1979

Kenneth Leech, *Youthquake*, Abacus 1976

Patrick Logan, *A Life to Be Lived*, Darton Longman and Todd 1989

Cilla McKenna, *Feel It*, Wild Goose 1989

Bernadette MacMahon, *Listening to Youth*, Dominican Publications 1987

Fred Milson, *Political Education*, Paternoster 1980

G. Keith Olson, *Counseling Teenagers*, Group Books 1984

Roger C. Palms, *The Jesus Kids*, SCM Press 1972

Lance Pierson, *The Pastoral Care of Young People*, Grove Books 1985

Donald C. Posterski, *Friendship: A Window on Ministry to Youth*, Project, Teen Canada 1985

Jim Rayburn III, *Dance Children, Dance*, Tyndale 1984

Wayne Rice, *Junior High Ministry*, Zondervan 1987

Lawrence O. Richards, *Youth Ministry*, Zondervan 1972

Gerard Rummery and Damian Lundy, *Growing into Faith*, Darton Longman and Todd 1982

St Mark's Sunday Club, *God, Fags and Teabags*, Sea Dream Music 1990

Peter Stow, *Youth in the City*, Hodder and Stoughton 1987

Nigel Sylvester, *God's Word in a Young World, The Story of Scripture Union*, SU 1984

Michael Warren, *Readings and Resources in Youth Ministry*, St Mary's Press 1987

———, *Youth and the Future of the Church*, Seabury 1982

———, *Youth, Gospel, Liberation*, Harper and Row 1984

Tricia Williams, *Christians in School*, SU 1985

Pip Wilson, *Gutter Feelings*, Marshall Pickering 1985